OXO

Children
love it

"You have
some, too."

"They're jolly well taking
Daily BOVRIL"

Published by Periplus Editions (HK) Ltd.
with editorial offices at
130 Joo Seng Road #06-01
Singapore 368357

ISBN: 962-593-979-2 (hardcover)
 0-7946-0089-1 (paperback)

Library of Congress
Card Number: 2002101478

Photo credits

All food and location photography by Ian Garlick. Additional photos Anthony Blake Photo Library: pp.12, 19, 24 & 33; Christopher Clunn Archives: pp.17, 22 & 23; Mary Evans Picture Library: pp.1 & 10; R. Tenison: pp.16 & 31; Robert Harding: pp.13, 14 & 15; Popperfoto: pp.8, 9 & 11.

Acknowledgments

The author, photographer and publishers would like to thank all the people involved in the prodcution of this publication, especially all of the owners, managers, chefs and staff of the restaurants included in these pages. Special thanks to the staff of Thomas Goode for their help with the styling of the food shots and for the loan of china, cutlery, glassware, and linen for the photographic shoot; and to Harrods for their generous sponsorship of the London Larder food section.

Distributed by

USA
Tuttle Publishing
Airport Industrial Park
364 Innovation Drive
North Clarendon, VT 05759-9436
Tel: (802) 773-8930
Fax: (802) 773-6993

Japan
Tuttle Publishing
RK Building 2nd Floor
2-13-10 Shimo-Meguro, Meguro-Ku
Tokyo 153 0064, Japan
Tel: (81-3) 5437-0171
Fax: (81-3) 5437-0755

Asia Pacific
Berkeley Books Pte. Ltd.
130 Joo Seng Road #06-01
Singapore 368357
Tel: (65) 6280-1330
Fax: (65) 6280-6290

First Edition
1 3 5 7 9 10 8 6 4 2
09 08 07 06 05 04 03 02
PRINTED IN SINGAPORE

THE FOOD OF
LONDON

A Culinary Tour of Classic British Cuisine

by Kathryn Hawkins
Photography by Ian Garlick

Additional Essays by Guy Dimond

Featuring recipes from the following restaurants:

Balls Brothers
Café Lazeez
Fortnum & Mason
The Fox & Anchor
Harrod's
Mr Wing
Simpson's-in-the-Strand
Snows on the Green

St. John
The Avenue
The Churchill Arms
The English Garden
The Ritz
The Seashell of Lisson Grove
Wiltons

PERIPLUS

Contents

the HONEST CABBAGE Restaurant

Part One: Food in London

London offers a wide range of culture and cuisine

by Kathryn Hawkins

In the last two decades of the twentieth century, London was transformed from a city of bland and uninspired culinary offerings to one of the greatest food capitals in the world. London has always been one of the best-loved cities in the world for its history, arts, and architecture but its food had never been a selling point. Recently, however, a culinary revolution has occurred. From pubs to smart restaurants, young, innovative British chefs are reinventing national favourites, foreign chefs are flocking to the city from all over the world, and immigrants from the West Indies, Africa, the Subcontinent, and the Far East have brought with them new ingredients and cooking styles, all of which has resulted in London's restaurant scene becoming the envy of the world.

Such a cosmopolitan flavor is due not only to recent developments, as, from the Roman conquest of the British Isles in AD 43 onwards, London has already been a magnet for travelers and settlers from around the globe. Migrants have brought their own unique culture and food, giving London the distinctive global melting pot of flavors and influences it has today; cuisines from all over the world can be found here, from the more common **Indian** and Chinese, to Middle Eastern, Africa, and South American.

Of course, the traditional cooking of Britain must not be forgotten, and there are endless places in which the food lover can sample local food—from fish and chips—a wicked combination of succulent white fish deep-fried in crisp batter and served with juicy, thick potato chips (fries) with malt vinegar—to the pie and mash, jellied eels, cockles, winkles, and curry houses of London's East End.

Many restaurants and pubs serve traditional Sunday lunches of roast beef and Yorkshire pudding, roast pork with apple sauce, or roast lamb and mint sauce, usually followed by apple pie and custard. A person with a hearty appetite could well start the day with an English breakfast, which typically consists of bacon, sausages, black pudding, fried or poached eggs, mushrooms, tomatoes, baked beans, and fried bread or toast. Some of the smallest cafés offer the best value for money.

Most people's inital thoughts of London are of the royal family, Buckingham Palace, the Tower of London, and the Houses of Parliament. Yet, behind all the tradition and the pomp and ceremony of formal London, there is a truly contemporary and cosmopolitan flavor to Britain's capital city. So, the next time you're in London town and you feel the pangs of hunger coming on, remember that you really are spoilt for choice!

Opposite:
The stylish café-bar at The Bluebird Restaurant on London's Kings Road.

A Culinary History of London

From the Romans to the present day

by Kathryn Hawkins

When the invading Roman legions reached Britain in AD 43, they introduced a variety of foods, such as peacocks, fallow deer, pheasants, figs, grapes, mulberries, walnuts, and chestnuts, as well as many of the herbs we cultivate today, including parsley, dill, mint, rosemary, and sage. They also brought vegetables, such as cabbages, onions, garlic, lettuce, turnips, and radishes. Add to this a list of culinary commodities like dates, almonds, olives, olive oil, ginger, pepper, and cinnamon, and it is clear to see their profound influence.

The Romans loved feasting; these diners are celebrating the feast of Hortensius.

In London (*Londinium* as it was called), some essential foods were locally produced. Salt, used for preserving and flavoring, came from the Thames estuary, and oysters were collected off the Kent coast. As well as trading with every part of the Roman Empire, London became the center for grain supplies, and for many centuries thereafter, locally grown grain and other farm produce could easily be brought to the capital from Kent, Essex, Surrey, and the Thames valley by river or road for trade and distribution.

The next important period in London's culinary history is between 1066 and 1520: medieval London. Sugar arrived in Britain courtesy of the Crusaders who brought it back from the East. Packed in white or brown cone shapes, it was very expensive and was regarded as a spice. Around 1290, citrus fruits began to arrive, and lemons were used fresh or pickled, as well as Seville oranges.

The range of imports and exports handled in London's harbors, wharves, and markets was impressive. They included strawberries, cherries, peas, beef, cod, mackerel, pepper, saffron, and cloves.

The earliest surviving recipe books date from this time. Fed up with salt, pepper, and the homegrown mustard and saffron used as flavorings, people were looking further afield to more exotic tastes, such as nutmeg, mace, cardamom, and cloves. These spices became highly sought after for their pungent, aromatic flavors. However, these spices were expensive as they were not imported direct and had to be purchased from markets in mainland Europe.

During the sixteenth century, the basic English food and diet remained the same as that of the previous era. Roast and boiled meat, fish and poultry, bread, ale, and wine formed a large part of the diet of the upper classes, and fruit and vegetables were less popular. In fact, during the great plague of 1569, the sale of fruit was banned in the streets because it was believed to cause sickness. After about 1580, however, there was a growth in market gardening, and by the turn of the next century, Londoners, who had always bought their fruit and vegetables from France and other parts of Europe, were able to buy from the orchards and gardens

Cardinal Wolsey presides over a banquet in the Presence Chamber at King Henry VII's Hampton Court palace.

of Kent, Surrey, Middlesex, Essex, and Hertfordshire. Even city gardeners were successful with only a few acres of land because demand was so high. For the more discerning and wealthy palate, new produce was still arriving from foreign shores— quinces, apricots, raspberries, red and black currants, melons, and pomegranates, as well as dried fruits and nuts.

This was the time of exploration and a number of rare and exotic foods began to arrive back in Elizabethan England: tomatoes from Mexico, kidney beans from Peru, turkeys and potatoes from Central America. Sugar grew in popularity, and from the 1540s a London refinery was busy making coarse crystals into tightly-packed white crystalline cones.

Sugar was used increasingly in preserving and for making all sorts of sweetmeats.

Coffee, chocolate, and tea arrived at the end of the century, and by the turn of the next, cookery books included recipes for dishes from Persia, Turkey, and Portugal, showing an ever-increasing fascination and demand for foreign flavors and delicacies; even ice had been introduced from the Continent at this time, as an idea for preserving.

By 1800, England was on the brink of the modern era, as the balance of power shifted from the land to the towns with the rise of the prosperous new middle classes, the development of newspapers and advertising, and the birth of a consumer society.

Right:
The beginnings of what has now become one of London's leading supermarket chains: J.Sainsbury's grocery store circa 1920.
Opposite:
A busy scene at Billingsgate fish market in London in 1935.

Cooking methods changed from open fire and spit roasting to flat iron griddles and plates on hobs. Roasting was the most important method of cooking, followed by boiling in a large cauldron, and then stewing and sauce-making over a gentle heat. Ice houses were built by the fashionable, and ice creams became a speciality. New recipe books of the period were written for the gentry and aimed to encourage them to aspire to a higher standard of living. Dinner table layouts, table manners and etiquette were featured, together with suggestions for different courses.

The style of eating also changed: simply flavored sauces and melted butter were served with meat dishes and vegetables alike; the pudding was invented—both savory and sweet; and sweet breads and cakes were popular as sugar came down in price.

Hothouses grew tomatoes, grapes, peaches, and salad vegetables. The advances and discoveries in agriculture led to cattle and livestock being bred for meat production all year round, and farm animals began to replace wild ones in the nation's diet.The big landowners gained control over the wild game on their land owing to the new land enclosure acts and the enforcement of severe gaming laws.

The poor, on the other hand, suffered in London as they did elsewhere. Thousands of rural laborers had lost their small homes and vegetable plots as a result of land enclosures, and were reduced to poverty and a diet of bread and potatoes. In London, working class families ate bread, potatoes, poor- quality meat and offal, fish, milk, tea, sugar, beer, butter, lard or dripping, and cheese. Supplies were inadequate and many were almost starving.

The making and taking of tea became an elegant ceremony amongst the middle and upper classes in London. In 1717, Thomas Twining had opened the first tea shop for ladies—there were already coffee shops for gentlemen—and in 1720, the first tea garden was opened in the old Vauxhall Gardens. This "fashion" soon spread, and tea eventually became an important social drink and industry.

However, as the eighteenth century drew to a close, food production increased in the United States, South America, Europe, India, and Australia. Transport became cheaper, and food processing techniques, such as freezing, canning, and bottling, were developed. Food prices fell, whilst wages remained the same, and consequently the poor were able to afford a better diet.

South London became an important center for manufacturing branded foods: Crosse and Blackwell, who made pickles, sauces, and condiments, had a factory in Southwark; Peak Frean and Company made biscuits in their Bermondsey factory; and Thomas Lipton started jam production.

In 1869, John Sainsbury opened his first grocery store in Drury Lane, offering a wider range of culinary goods than ever before, and aimed at the new middle classes. This store became the predecessor of the modern-day supermarket. By the early 1900s, several were operating in Britain and the "multiple ownership" culture was born. It wasn't until 1949 that the first self-service shops were opened, and supermarkets only became commonplace in the 1960s.

By the outbreak of World War I in 1914, Britain was dependent on imports for half of all its food. Shipping losses during wartime began to cause food shortages. Strict pricing controls were enforced, and in 1918 rationing was introduced with the result that both the rich and poor were eating the same food. Ironically, it enabled many working class people to have a better diet than prior to the restrictions.

In 1939, with the outbreak of World War II, the Government began another system of food rationing which remained in operation until 1954. Rations were strictly calculated to ensure that the population remained healthy. Many everyday foods became unobtainable, and ingenious substitutes were developed for eggs, cheese, bananas, and chocolate.

An important factor in London's recent culinary history is its migrant population. It has seen its fair share of migrant workers throughout its history, but the twentieth century witnessed the largest ever rise in its immigrant population. In the 1920s and 1930s, the Irish established their own community in West London. Many Poles arrived in postwar London, mainly servicemen fleeing occupied France, as well as those who had been in Germany as prisoners or conscripts. Many Italians also came to London and successfully merged into the local communities, opening up bistros and pasta restaurants. Greek Cypriots started arriving in the 1920s, bringing with them their flair for catering.

After 1945 West Indians were recruited to work for public service companies. Brixton and Notting Hill are well known for their colorful markets selling exotic produce from the Caribbean homelands. The relaxation of emigration restrictions in India and Pakistan in the 1960s created a rush of migrants, and many settled in London. Today, Brick Lane is synonymous with curry houses and Asian cuisine, and Southall and Tooting are popular Asian centers. Other areas of London famous for their ethnic populations are Golders Green and Muswell Hill for the Jewish community, Soho for London's Chinatown, and the Edgware Road for the Arab quarter. London is now a truly cosmopolitan city, and it is possible to eat out in restaurants from all corners of the globe.

Opposite:
Advertisement posters from the 1930s for two popular meat extract drinks, Bovril and OXO.

Feasts, Festivals, and Celebrations

*Contemporary London food is still influenced
by the traditional feasts of the past*

by Kathryn Hawkins

Throughout the year, all over Britain, festivals and celebrations take place to commemorate specific events or to maintain religious, pagan, historical or sporting traditions. There are also quite a few unusual and often superstitious traditions which take place in London. Many traditions involve feasting and the preparation and baking of special food for the occasion. Londoners also have their own festivals which relate specifically to the city's multi-ethnic society and the individual cultures that make London so cosmopolitan.

One of the traditions carried out in the theater world occurs on January 6 at the Drury Lane Theater, where the cast eat cake and drink wine as directed in the will of a comedian called Baddeley, who died in 1795. Another less well known event takes place two days later on January 8, or the first Sunday after, when the Chaplain of Clowns preaches a sermon and recites a prayer over the grave of the great clown Joseph Grimaldi. A wreath is also laid. This ceremony takes place by the former St. James's church in Pentonville. In January or February, depending on the lunar calendar, London's Chinatown becomes alive with the sights and sounds of Chinese New Year celebrations. Gerrard Street in Soho (in London's West End) is decked out in symbolic red and gold; lanterns and lights are hung from windows and street lamps, and the streets are packed with people all eager to see the Dragon dancers performing to the Chinese drummers and musicians. All the shops, bars and restaurants prepare themselves for a busy few days at this time of year.

Depending on when Easter falls in the calendar, the day before the beginning of Lent, Shrove Tuesday, heralds the start of a forty-day period of fasting for Christians, which ends on Easter Sunday. Although nowadays, few people observe Lent, nearly everyone eats pancakes, and it is now usually referred to as Pancake Day. Pancake races are held, in which competitors have to run with a pancake in a skillet, flipping it up in the air and catching it again. If a pancake is dropped, the participant is disqualified.

Opposite:
Most families sit down to a large Christmas lunch of roast turkey; roast potatoes; roasted seasonal vegetables, such as parsnips; and dessert of rich Christmas pudding and brandy butter.
Left:
Pancake racers on Shrove Tuesday. This tradition is still practised all over England to mark the beginning of Lent.

On the fourth Sunday in Lent, Mothering Sunday is celebrated. In medieval times it was the day when people traveled to their Mother Church or Cathedral to worship. It wasn't until the mid-seventeenth century that it became linked to the family. A favorite bake was the Simnel cake—a fruit cake with a marzipan topping. The cake is decorated with twelve marzipan balls to represent Christ's apostles and is a popular addition to the Easter tea table.

One of the oldest Druid ceremonies takes place on March 21st on Tower Hill to celebrate the spring equinox. Later in the year (around September 23), they meet again to celebrate the autumn equinox.

Good Friday is the most solemn day in the Christian calendar, and church services are held all over London. After morning service at St. Bartholomew the Great in Smithfield, 21 widows of the parish collect a bun and sixpence from the top of a tomb in the churchyard. Two days later, Easter is celebrated, marking the end of Lent, and it is an opportunity for families to gather for a feast of roast lamb. The shops are stocked with Easter eggs and chocolate bunnies. In London's Battersea Park, the annual Easter Parade is held.

The feast of St. George, patron saint of England, falls on April 23. George is believed to have been a Christian centurion who was martyred by the Roman Emperor Diocletian at Lydda in Palestine around AD 303. He took on a symbolic importance to the English when Richard the Lionheart recaptured the church at Lydda during the Crusades. In 1415, his feast day was declared a national religious festival in England after the Battle of Agincourt.

To commemorate the Queen's official birthday in June, crowds gather to watch the Trooping the Color at Horse Guards Parade. The Queen inspects her Guards as they march past and then proceeds to Buckingham Palace at the head of them. This heralds the beginning of the "summer season". The race meeting at Royal Ascot in the third week of June has a strict dress code: men wear lounge or morning suits with top hats, and the women dress up, too, especially on "Ladies Day" when they wear their most extravagant headwear. The Wimbledon lawn tennis championship takes place in the last week of June and first week of July. Tonnes of strawberries are served with cream, and gallons of Pimms and champagne are drunk.

Meanwhile, at the Henley Royal Regatta, blazer-clad men and women in floating dresses picnic on the tables and chairs set out in front of their Rolls-Royces or Bentleys!

At the Bank Holiday weekend at the end of August, a carnival takes place in London's Notting Hill. Staged by the West Indian community, the participants parade in colorful costumes and dance to pulsating reggae rhythms. The streets fill up with thousands of people and the partying continues well into the night. Street vendors sell West Indian foods.

As summer fades away, Harvest festival is celebrated in churches with altars laden with sheaths of corn and baskets of fruits and vegetables.

On November 5, 1605, Guy Fawkes, a Catholic, was found in the cellars of the Houses of Parliament, planning to ignite barrels of gunpowder later that day when the Protestant King James I was to open Parliament. Every year, to commemorate the foiling of the plot, children make replica 'guys' which are burnt on bonfires. Firework displays and bonfire parties are held all over Britain.

As the year draws to a close, the shops are piled high with Christmas goodies gifts. Houses and streets all over the country are decorated with lights and Christmas trees. London's Regent Street and Oxford Street are illuminated, and Trafalgar Square is

Revellers in the streets at London's Notting Hill Carnival, the largest carnival in Europe.

adorned by a huge lit Christmas tree, a present from the people of Norway. On Christmas Day, brave members of the Serpentine Swimming Club plunge into the icy river to race for the Peter Pan Cup. On December 31, people gather in Trafalgar Square and at the London Eye to welcome in the New Year. As the chimes of Big Ben strike midnight, they join hands and sing "Auld Lang Syne" and the celebrations for the New Year begin.

Eels, Pie, and Mash

For a taste of real East End Cockney food,
you can still savor pie and mash

by Charlotte Hunt

Pie, mash, and liquor, together with jellied or stewed eels, are often perceived as Cockney food —a speciality of London's East End. It's true that today the majority of the distinctive eel, pie and mash houses are situated in this part of the capital, and many of the original establishments, from the 1840s onwards, sprung up here. However, just after World War II, you could eat this traditional dish in at least 130 shops all over the city from Soho to Bermondsey.

Sadly only a fraction remain, as the arrival of fast food and worldwide gastronomic influences have brought about the partial demise of this traditional fare. However, the trade is still dominated by three families—the Cookes, Manzes, and Kellys, whose history is an important part of the pie and mash story.

No one knows who invented the dish or opened the first shop. We do know that in Victorian London, street vendors sold eel pies, providing cheap yet nutritious food for the poor. These were eaten with parsley sauce, spiced with chilies and vinegar, which survives today as the famous green liquor.

Ealing eel and pie shop that serves traditional pie, mash, and eels to Londoners.

The eels originally came from Holland and legend suggests that John Antink, a Dutch trader, sold the fish from a makeshift shop, although Kelly's Trades Directory doesn't mention this business until 1880. However, we can verify the existence of an eel and pie shop in 1844 at 101 Union Street, London SE1. Here a man called Henry Blanchard sold meat, eel, and fruit pies for a penny as well as live eels and mashed potato. By 1874, Kelly's listed 33 eel and pie shops, and their success no doubt encouraged Robert Cooke to open his own establishment in Clerkenwell in 1889, officially launching the Cooke eel and pie empire. Staff wore white aprons, and a typical shop had white-tiled walls, marble tables, wooden benches, and huge mirrors. There were two large windows on either side of the front door, which opened up to provide a takeout service. The customers spat eel bones onto the sawdust-covered floor, although everything was scrupulously clean and the interiors had a simple elegance and charm. Inspired by his success, Cooke swiftly opened up a second shop in Watney Street E1 while his wife opened a third shop in Hoxton Street N1. Another pie and mash pioneer, Michaele Manze, arrived from Ravello, Italy, in 1878. He soon became friends with Robert Cooke, married his daughter Ada and opened up the first Manze shop in Bermondsey.

Finally, Samuel Kelly, an Irish immigrant, opened his Bethnal Green Road shop in 1915 and by the 1940s the business had expanded to include four other shops, all within a mile and a half radius.

Pie and mash survived the World Wars despite conscription of the white working class males who made up the majority of regular customers. The shops upheld their reputation for supplying good reasonably priced food although eels were scarce and eel pies largely disappeared from the menu.

Rewards were justly reaped when the wars were over and boys in their demob suits flooded the shops desperate for a taste of their favorite cuisine.

Pie and mash enjoyed huge popularity and for the next few years London's thriving docks, factories and markets guaranteed an enormous demand.

In the 1950s, rising rents forced many factories to move out to newly built towns in Essex. The pie and mash clientele moved with them and the number of London shops decreased to the present-day figure of around thirty.

Shrewd local businessmen opened up similar eating houses in the new towns as well as nearby seaside resorts, ensuring that pie and mash was no longer exclusive to London. However, the original proprietors still claim that customers travel for miles to enjoy the dish in its "proper" form.

The Cookes still have four shops, and the

A live eel prior to preparation in the kitchens of F.Cookes pie and mash shop in Broadway Market.

Manzes, who proved themselves the true entrepreneurs of the business with 14 shops, still have five branches. Five Kelly's shops also continue to thrive, serving East End regulars and visitors as they have done for 86 years.

Many London families remain loyal pie and mash enthusiasts and the meal has recently been discovered by the middle classes intrigued by this slice of culinary history. Hopefully, the appeal of cheap, tasty sustaining food eaten in historic surroundings will survive.

Dining Out in London

In London's ethnically diverse eateries,
you can eat truly cosmopolitan food

by Guy Dimond

London just isn't like the rest of Britain. It's still true that finding a good meal in rural Britain—or even some of the larger cities—takes sleuth-like skills and a well-thumbed copy of The Good Food Guide, but London has become a center of excellence which is now on a par with the best food cities in the world, such as New York, San Francisco, and Sydney. And this has happened within the last 15 years or so. If you haven't visited London for a few years, then you're in for a big shock.

London always had the makings of a great restaurant city, but for some reason it just didn't take off until the 1980s. London's a wealthy city; it has a huge population (over seven million people, depending on where you consider the boundaries of "London" to lie); and it's a multicultural city, so there's a score of diverse communities who have brought their food cultures to the city. Londoners are less conservative in their dining habits than other British people or, indeed, other Europeans. And, of course, London doesn't just comprise British-born people. Britain has long been a member of the European Union; as more European countries join, chefs from Stockholm to Lisbon are able to work legally in London. Equally, young chefs from Commonwealth countries, such as Australia and New Zealand, find it easy to get work (for a couple of years at least). And when Hong Kong was returned to China in 1997, many of the best Cantonese chefs decided it was time to move to London, making London's *dim sum* some of the best you'll find anywhere. Chefs apart, London itself is an ethnically diverse city: by the year 2050, more than half of London's population will have one or both parents of Asian or African heritage.

London's multiculturalism is only a precondition of it being a great city for eating out—what has really driven the restaurant boom is the growth in disposable income. Between 1986 and 2001, there was an increase in the average household income of around 40 percent. This occurred at the same time as a drop in the cost of living (in real terms).

The Warrington hotel, formerly owned, in the late 1800s, by the Church of England, now a bar and restaurant.

first of the grand designs was Quaglino's, which Conran modeled on the Parisian brasserie *La Coupole*. It was spectacular; it was pricey; it also served good food. Conran judged that Londoners were ready to appreciate the theater and fun of eating out, and were no longer just concerned about portion sizes and price. Conran continues to build an empire of expensive but well-managed restaurants to this day.

A revolution was also happening at the other end of the price scale. Cheap fast food in London had previously been dominated by second-rate pizza and pasta places, or kebabs and burgers; there weren't even many good sandwich bars. Then, in 1986, Pret à Manger opened its first sandwich bar, selling ready-made but high-quality sandwiches, and now there's one on every major street in central London. In the 1990s, espresso chains took over the high streets, though these are more clearly modeled on (or even owned by) State-side chains, such as Starbucks. Asian food in London had previously been dominated by Chinese takeaways and Indian curry houses, but in 1992 Wagamama created a huge stir when it opened its first branch. Food from the Far East had previously been "ghettoized", but Wagamama's intriguing mix of Japanese-style noodles mixed with Southeast Asian flavors was a huge hit. The restaurant is cheap and theatrical. The huge, minimally designed space features shared bench seating, fast turnaround, and quick-moving lines (no bookings are taken). Alan Yau, its creator, sold the growing chain, then went on to set up Busaba Eathai (which does a similar thing with Thai food) and, in 2001, opened Hakkasan (a very glamorous Chinese

This might be hard to believe as London is still the most expensive city in Europe, but Londoners simply have more money than they've ever had. And think back to the 1980s; for a short while, Greed Was Good, and the previous British reserve about throwing money around in bars and restaurants evaporated.

Restaurateurs such as Sir Terence Conran sniffed the change in mood and realized that the time was right to build lavish, opulent restaurants. One of the restaurant serving *dim sum* at lunchtime).

Besides the mass-market budget restaurants and the big names like Conran, there is also a quieter revolution going on in London's kitchens. It started a long time ago, arguably with the cookery writing of Elizabeth David in the 1960s. However, it took until the 1980s for her Mediterranean approach of using the finest ingredients and preparing them simply to start appearing on smart restaurant menus. Previously, London's top chefs had been pursuing the Michelin route—using the decades-old French approach of lots of butter, cream, meat, and reduced sauces. French *haute cuisine* was becoming less appealing to a more health-conscious public.

Early pioneers of the so-called "Modern British" cooking included Alastair Little opening in Soho in 1984, and, also in 1984, Sally Clarke who introduced "Cal-Ital" cooking to London (having learned her approach from Alice Waters in Berkeley, California). Soon their style of cooking became the norm. However, the term "Modern British" is a misnomer; there's not much that's typically British about ingredients like lemongrass or harissa, or cooking techniques like char-grilling or searing. The term "Modern European" is now usually preferred (and it's much the same as "Contemporary American" or "Modern Australian" cooking). If you singled out London's top 100 restaurants, around 70 could be categorized as "Modern European".

The British still like their pubs, even though by the 1980s many London pubs were owned by a handful of brewery chains selling mass-produced, insipid, or badly-kept ales and lagers. The reaction to this was not a groundswell of people clamoring

The Chef at Satsuma, in Soho, shows off a bento box.

for real ales; instead they switched to other drinks—bottled beers and pre-mixed alcopops—where at least the quality was consistent. A few pubs continue to champion real ales and even microbrewed ales, but one of the biggest changes is that London's pub owners have realized that there's money to be made by serving customers good food as well as drink. One of the first and most influential gastropubs was The Eagle in Farringdon. It strived to

If you want the most stylish, chic restaurant interiors you can imagine, then New Yorker Ian Schrager's in town with his Sanderson and St. Martin's Lane hotels—though I'd recommend just popping in for a drink to look around, as the restaurants are fantastically expensive. If you want to see where the Brit Art crowd go to discuss their next "project", then the Shoreditch/Hoxton area is the place to be. And, of course, if you just want a good meal, there's no shortage of great new restaurants. Check out the weekly *Time Out* magazine or the *Time Out Eating & Drinking Guide* for a round-up of the capital's best places.

Picking the best places to eat and drink is a bit like chasing a will-o'-the-wisp, but here are a few places I would recommend:
- Breakfast at Smiths of Smithfield (first floor café).
- *Dim sum* in Chinatown or Queensway, served in a dozen restaurants from noon until 5pm
- St. John restaurant, for its extraordinary take on British food—be warned, there's lots of offal.
- The Sugar Club in Soho. It's not cheap, but it's worth it just to see just how good fusion food can be.
- Like Indian food? Don't go to Brick Lane, which is totally overrated—there's not a single good "Indian" restaurant there. Go instead to Drummond Street near Euston, for the vegetarian dishes of cafés like Diwana or Ravi Shankar. If you have more money to spend, and like seafood, Rasa Samudra, north of Oxford Street, has no peers.

be a happy mix of both pub and dining area, so there was no pressure to just eat or drink; the beers were good, there was even a decent wine list, and the cooking was an unusual style of Iberian-inspired dishes. It was a huge hit, sparking a wave of spin-off gastropubs and restaurants, such as the muchlauded Moro. London's gastropubs go from strength to strength. Some of the best meals I've eaten this year have been in gastropubs, not chi-chi restaurants.

London is a genuinely exciting place to eat out, because there's something for everyone. If you like budget "ethnic" restaurants, there are delightful cafés like the Sudanese Mandola in Notting Hill, the Vietnamese Viet Hoa in Hoxton, the Burmese Mandalay on the Edgware Road, or the Turkish Mangal in Dalston.

TODAY'S MARKET OF
DUTCH VEAL

	PER KILO
LEG VEAL	13·80
ROLLED VEAL with kidney	21·60
LOIN CHOPS	21·00
VEAL ESCALOPE	23·10
KNUCKLE VEAL	13·80
PIE VEAL	10·35
FILLET VEAL	26·45
BREAST VEAL	N/A
MINCE VEAL	4·70
OSSO BUCO	13·80
MEDAILLION VEAL	26·45

TODAY'S MARKET OF
SCOTCH BEEF

	PER KILO
MINCE	5·50
BRAISING STEAK	6·40
RUMP STEAK	14·00
ENTRECOTE STEAK	25·85
FILLET STEAK	32·00
TOPSIDE	9·90
TOP RUMP	9·90
SILVERSIDE	7·70
ROLLED SIRLOIN	22·20
SIRLOIN on the Bone	N/A
BEEF OLIVES	10·35
MINUTE STEAK	24·64
SALT SILVERSIDE	8·60
TOP RIB	N/A
BRISKET	4·85
SLOW ROAST	6·41

Food and Drink from Scotland
Fillet Steak
Promotional Price
£25.00 per Kg

Food and Drink from Scotland
Rump Steak
Promotional Price
£12.00 per Kg

Specially Selected SCOTCH BEEF

Part Two: Cooking in London

*Some familiar and more unusual utensils and ingredients
which are found in the well-stocked London kitchen and larder*

The tools of the trade for the average London cook include some specialist items that are invaluable for preparing the more traditional British meals.

A potato peeler, sharp vegetable knife, and potato masher are essential whereas a deep-fryer with an inner basket is useful for cooking chips (fries). Asparagus may be cooked in a special, tall pan with an inner basket, which allows the delicate tips to cook in the steam.

For fruit, use a corer to get a clean cut from apples and pears. Other gadgets include pincers for hulling soft fruits, and stoners for pitting cherries, and zesters and canelling knives for stripping the rind from citrus fruits.

For roasting meat and poultry, there is a variety of baking pans; a meat thermometer is useful to check whether joints are cooked. Before cooking, some joints need to be tied, and a trussing needle will help you do this neatly. For lean joints or delicate poultry, a larding needle threads fat under the skin to prevent the meat drying out as it cooks.

A long "fish kettle" is perfect for cooking whole salmon and other large fish; a steamer will enable you to cook smaller fish and fillets to perfection. Use a fish slice to remove the cooked fish.

Many traditional recipes involve baking, and there are several useful dishes, pans, and molds. Pies with a firm crust can be made in special spring-clipped metal molds, whilst shallower ones are baked in ceramic pie dishes. Use a pie funnel to let the steam escape; traditional ones are shaped like birds. Sweet and savory puddings can be made in metal basins and molds, or strong ceramic bowls. Spherical molds are used for rich, fruity Christmas puddings, while others are steamed in a pudding cloth or cheesecloth tied with string over a pan of simmering water. Yorkshire pudding can be made in roasting pans, muffin pans, or individual molds.

Many cakes are cooked in shallow round cake pans called Victoria Sandwich tins, often nonstick for convenience or made of aluminum. Deeper pans are useful for heavier cakes and fruit cakes.

Jellies are made in metal, glass, or plastic molds and dishes in many unusual shapes and sizes, often served with a scoop of dairy ice-cream.

Spices are important flavorings, so an electric grinder is good for crushing whole spices—or use a pestle and mortar. Spice mills are useful for grinding peppercorns and harder spices. Whole nutmegs can be grated on small metal graters. Use a large metal preserving pan for making jams and jellies. A jelly bag is useful for straining fruit, while a thermometer takes the guesswork out of jam making. A jam funnel will help prevent mess when bottling preserves. For stockist information for kitchen equipment, see page 138.

Asparagus steamer

Ice-cream scoop

Nutmeg grater

Fruit corer/peeler

Potato masher

BREADS AND BAKERY PRODUCTS

One of London's favorite fast foods is the sandwich, and, as we've already established, cheese and hams are popular fillings. However, using the right bread can make all the difference to the finished product. There are many varieties available but a few standard loaves and other bakery products that are exclusively British. Specialist bakeries make and sell their own breads and products, whilst supermarkets and local shops offer a wider selection for convenience. Here are some you may see:

BLOOMER: The English name for a long white loaf with rounded ends, slashed diagonally with evenly spaced deepish cuts just before baking. It is perfect for slicing thickly and making a chunky sandwich, colloquially called a "doorstop"!

CHELSEA BUN: A loose spiral bun with fruit and spice, squared off at the sides. It is well baked and golden, and sugar crusted. Chelsea buns have been known since the eighteenth century and were originally sold from a cook's shop known as the Bun House, situated in London's Chelsea. They can be eaten cold or slightly warmed, split and spread with butter.

COBURG or COB: A popular English crusty loaf made from all-purpose white flour. It is rounded in shape and the crust can be cut in several ways: a cross, one spreading cut, a checkerboard design, or punctured with small holes made with a thin, rounded piece of wood. This loaf will slice thinly, making a more delicate sandwich.

COTTAGE: This consists of two round loaves of white bread baked one on top of the other, the top being smaller than the bottom. It has a deep gold crust which gives it a less crumbly texture than other breads, so it is good for slicing but makes an unusual shaped sandwich!

CRUMPET: A type of thick, perforated pancake made from a thick yeasty batter. Cooked on a lightly greased hot plate called a griddle, crumpets are only turned briefly and so the underside is rich golden and smooth, whilst the top is pale and full of holes. They're often served at tea-time, lightly toasted and spread with butter and jam.

ENGLISH MUFFIN: A round yeasted bread bun enriched with milk and butter. It is usually cooked on a griddle which gives it a flat, golden-browntop and bottom with a white band around the middle. The texture is light and spongy. For serving, muffins are toasted on both sides and then split open, thickly buttered, and sandwiched back together.

FARMHOUSE: An English loaf shape which is short, thick, and rounded oblong in shape, sometimes with the name impressed on the sides. It can be made from white, wholemeal, or granary flour, and is perfect for slicing.

GRANARY: This loaf takes its name from the flour that is composed of mixed brown wheat and rye with malted, cracked wheat grains. It is soft in texture with a sweet, malty flavor, and can be baked in many shapes. This bread adds its own texture and flavor to a sandwich.

VIENNA: A glazed, bright golden, crusty white loaf cooked with the aid of steam in the oven to give a very light texture. It is usually a pointed oval in shape with a central slash down its length.

CHEESE

The British love cheese, and it is included in many dishes: grated to flavor a sauce; added to stuffings and fillings; grilled or baked as a topping for gratins and pies, or simply served as a filling for sandwiches, with salad or bread and pickle. There are hundreds of English cheeses, all with their own characteristics, flavors, and uses.

CHEDDAR: This hard cheese has a close texture and varies in color from pale straw to golden orange. Its full, nutty flavor varies in strength according to the time it is left to mature. The strongest, tangy Farmhouse Cheddars are made from the best-quality milk. Cheddar is added to cooked dishes for a really cheesy flavor, and is the traditional cheese for a ploughman's lunch

CHESHIRE: The oldest British cheese has a slightly crumbly texture and mellow flavor. It is mellow, creamy with a salty bite, and may be white or colored orange with a vegetable dye. It is good for grilling and makes an excellent accompaniment to semi-sweet biscuits and fruit. A blue-veined variety is highly sought after; it has a rich, creamy, strong, tangy flavor.

DERBY: This hard, close, smooth-textured cheese is white in color, with a mild, clean, fresh flavor. You can also buy green-marbled Sage Derby.

DOUBLE GLOUCESTER: Golden orange with a firm, smooth texture and delicate creamy flavor, this is ideal for cooking or eating.

LANCASHIRE: A white, soft-textured, crumbly cheese with a mild flavor. Try crumbling it over vegetables and bakes before grilling, or grate and sprinkle on top of soups and casseroles.

LEICESTER: This rich russet-coloured cheese has a mild, mellow flavor and open texture. It makes an excellent Welsh Rarebit (see page 96). It dries out quickly so purchase it in small quantities.

STILTON: Referred to as the "king of cheeses", its distinctive blue veining is caused by a mold being introduced into the cheese during manufacturing. Between the veining, a mature Stilton should be a rich creamy color, with a strong but subtle flavor. It is best appreciated eaten simply with savory crackers and accompanied by a glass of port. White Stilton is more crumbly with a milder, slightly sour flavor. It is similar to Greek Feta cheese and makes a good alternative. It is often flavored with chopped apricots or nuts.

STINKING BISHOP: This is one of a number of strangely named cheese. It is made in Gloucester and has a soft white rind, like Brie, which is washed in brine, giving the cheese a strong pungent smell—hence the first part of its name. However, the second part is more uncertain! The cheese is semi-hard in texture with a distinctive unusual flavor—slightly salty and nutty—well worth trying if you see some.

WENSLEYDALE: This mild, white cheese has a close texture but crumbles easily. Its creamy, mild, salty flavor goes well with fruit. It is traditionally served with a slice of apple pie or fruit cake.

YARG: This was developed in Cornwall in the 1970s by the Gray family (their name spelt backwards was given to the cheese!). Ripened with mold, it is semi-hard with a creamy, fresh, almost lemony taste. The cheese is wrapped in nettle leaves to give the rind a powdery gray pattern.

FISH AND SHELLFISH

Many traditional British dishes have fish as the main ingredient. The most famous and oldest takeout meal is fish and chips. Here are some of the most familiar fish enjoyed in London today:

COCKLES: These are usually sold out of their shells in jars, preserved in brine or vinegar, although cooked cockles may be sold loose. Beige and orange in color, they can be mixed into fish pies or may be eaten as a popular East End snack, sold in small pots by street vendors.

COD: A classic fish available all year round, cod has thick, white, flaky flesh with a light flavor. It is traditionally fried in batter and is a favorite in most fish and chip shops, but it is also used in fish pies and fish cakes or is simply grilled or baked with butter.

DOVER SOLE: A very popular flat fish in the early twentieth century, when it was simply grilled and served with butter. Nowadays it is expensive and is at its best in spring and summer, about three days after being caught. The best Dover sole weigh about 14–16 ounces (400–450 g). Grilling is still the best way to cook them, seasoned with a little black pepper and sprinkled with lemon juice and chopped parsley.

HADDOCK: A reasonably priced fish with flaky white flesh, this is a much-loved favorite in England and Scotland. It is usually coated in batter or breadcrumbs and deep-fried, but is also good simply poached with its skin on to prevent it breaking up. It is also smoked and may be colored with natural yellow dye. It is most popularly used in the breakfast dish kedgeree, mixed with curried rice and eggs. If very fresh, it can be served raw in wafer-thin slices like smoked salmon.

LEMON SOLE: This flat fish has a softer texture and less flavor than Dover sole. Available all year round, it is sold on the bone, which is the best way to cook it as it holds up well and the flesh comes away easily. Simply grill with black pepper, butter, and lemon juice.

SALMON: Known as the king of fish, salmon is found in rivers all over Europe, Iceland, Canada, and the East Coast of America, but Scottish salmon are believed to be the finest. They can grow very large, but smaller ones have a better flavor. A good fish has a small head with a silvery blue body and distinctive black markings. The flesh is oily and orangey pink. Wild salmon are becoming rarer, and most of the salmon available now is farmed. It is a versatile fish and can be bought whole, in cutlets, steaks, or fillets. Grill it, fry it in its own juices, roast it, poach or steam it. It is best served simply, hot or cold, with a creamy sauce or mayonnaise.

WHITEBAIT: A term used for a mix of the fry of herring, pilchard, and sprats. Small and silvery, they used to be readily caught in British rivers including the Thames. A dish of deep-fried whitebait with lemon, salt, and cayenne was a popular Cockney feast. They are at their best from February to July, but are now almost always frozen. The flesh is oily and tasty, but they are very delicate so rinse with care and pat dry using kitchen paper. Dust lightly with seasoned flour and then deep-fry or shallow-fry. Serve simply in the Cockney tradition.

HAM

Pork is widely used in hams and gammons, which are eaten in sandwiches with mustard or pickle, or with salads or a hunk of cheese.

BRADENHAM: A well-known ham from Wiltshire. After dry-curing, it is placed in molasses, brown sugar, and spices and turned and basted daily. It is hung to dry and mature for several months before smoking until the outside is black. It can be salty and requires soaking. It has a sweet, delicate flavor and is often served cold.

DEVONSHIRE: These hams may be smoked or un-smoked and cured for cooking. They are very lean and succulent with a clean, pure flavor.

SUFFOLK: This is cured by rubbing salt and salt-petre into the surface, then covering in a mixture of old ale, treacle, brown sugar, and spices. It is turned and basted for a month, then hung and matured for four months. It can be boiled, baked or braised and has a full but mild flavor.

WILTSHIRE: This ham dates back hundreds of years. It has lean meat with a mild flavor.

YORK: The traditional ham of England is dry-cured, then baked and matured. Green York ham is dry-cured, washed and matured in a calico bag for six months. It needs cooking before eating.

MEAT PRODUCTS

Some of the more curious meat products include:

BLACK PUDDING: Served at a traditional English breakfast. This north England speciality is made from pork and pig's blood. It is usually sliced and fried, and its rich, savory, spicy flavor goes partic-ularly well with fried apple rings.

HASLET: Cooked, brined pork and offal made in loaves. It is cut and thinly sliced and used as a sand-wich filling or as a sliced meat. Beige-pink with a dark brown edge, it has a salty flavor seasoned with black pepper and sometimes sage.

POLONY: A mixture of lean and fat raw pork which is cooked and sold in a bright red skin. The meat is pale pink and has a mild cured-pork flavor, lightly spiced and smoked.

SAVELOY: Made from minced, smoked and cured pork mixed with cereal and seasoning, this is deep-fried, sometimes in batter.

SAUSAGES

One of the great British favorites is the sausage, and there are many different flavors. Sausages are bought fresh and then grilled, fried or baked.

CAMBRIDGE: Sausages flavored with sage, cayenne, and nutmeg.

CUMBERLAND: Made of coarsely cut pork, this is spicier than most sausages. It is sold by length from a long coil. It's usually baked or pan cooked, twisted into a large spiral.

GLOUCESTER: Made from Gloucestershire Old Spot pig, these sausages are very large.

LINCOLNSHIRE: Flavored with sage and thyme.

MANCHESTER: Sausages flavored with sage, cloves, nutmeg, and ginger.

NEWMARKET: A moderately spicy sausage with a few herbs, made to a secret family recipe.

OXFORD: Made from pork, veal and beef with sage, nutmeg, pepper, and sometimes herbs.

WILTSHIRE: Ginger and other seasonings.

YOKRSHIRE: Nutmeg, cloves, and cayenne.

Thyme

Tarragon

Chives

Sage

HERBS

Throughout the centuries, various herbs have typically been used to flavor many traditional British dishes. Elaborate herb gardens have been cultivated by aristocrats and wealthy landowners for decades, and most Britons with a garden or back yard, some patio tubs, a roof garden or even a window box grow at least one type of culinary herb or another. Here is a list of some of the most frequently used herbs in the Londoner's kitchen, accompanied by information on how these herbs are most commonly used:

BAY LEAVES: These are also known as "sweet bay" or "sweet laurel". The aromatic leaves of this bush or tree are an essential flavoring in the kitchen and a basic herb in European cooking. The glossy green leaves can be used fresh or dried and have a strong balsamic taste which fades with age. Bay leaves are always part of a "bouquet garni" and are used as a flavoring for fish, chicken, and meat, and also in pickles and preserves. The flavor lends itself to citrus fruits and berries, so try adding it to fruit compotes for an alternative flavor.

CHIVES: Native to most of Europe, the chive is an onion with clover-like lilac flowers and fine, tubular grass-like leaves. The flowers can be used in salads, but it is the leaves that are more commonly used. Snipped chives can be added to hot dishes at the last moment as they wilt very quickly and lose their lovely fresh green color. Chives are particularly useful whenever you need a subtle onion flavor. Snipped into short lengths or left longer for a more graphic effect, they make a very attractive garnish. They are also excellent for flavoring cheese dishes and many egg recipes, especially scrambled eggs. Try replacing the onion in coleslaw salad with chives for a less penetrating flavor. Dried chives are always a poor substitute for fresh.

DILL: Native to southern Europe, dill has been adopted by Scandinavia and is widely used there. It is an attractive, feathery herb with thread-like blue-green leaves. The taste is mildly sweet and very aromatic. Dill makes a good garnish although it wilts quickly. It goes particularly well with cucumber and smoked fish, such as salmon or mackerel. You can add finely chopped dill to vegetable and fish soups, potato salads, cream cheese, eggs, and grilled meats. It is also good boiled with baby new potatoes. The aromatic, flattish oval seeds are also used in some pickles and with fish.

MINT: This is one of the best-loved herbs in English cookery. Indeed, it is almost impossible to imagine eating some roast lamb or lamb chops without the traditional accompaniment of mint sauce. There are many varieties of mint, of which spearmint is the one most favored by cooks. It is used not only mixed with sugar and vinegar when making mint sauce but also for flavoring fresh garden peas and new potatoes. Just add a sprig or two of fresh mint to the pan before cooking. Spearmint sprigs are the finishing touch to a tall glass of Pimm's at a summer gathering. Other varieties of mint include the following: applemint (used in salads), bergamot mint (usually citrus-scented), Eau de Cologne mint (used in fruit jellies), ginger mint (the perfect accompaniment to melon), and the distinctive scented pineapple mint.

PARSLEY: This is the most commonly used herb in European and American cooking; it is second only to cilantro (fresh coriander) in the rest of the world. There are two widely known varieties: the curly leaf parsley which has dark green, dense, crinkly leaves; and the single-leaf Continental or flat-leaf parsley, which has a superior flavor—clean and fresh tasting. Parsley freezes well but when dried it tends to taste like sweet hay.

It adds more flavor when added to a dish at the end of cooking and is good chopped and mixed into salads. Parsley sauce is a traditional accompaniment for fish and cooked ham. Parsley is also a commonly used garnish for many savory dishes, either in whole sprigs or coarsely or finely chopped.

ROSEMARY: One of the commonest wild plants of dry Mediterranean regions, rosemary has been embraced enthusiastically by the British and is a strongly aromatic herb with distinct overtones of camphor. It was introduced by the Romans to Britain and is now widely used in many classic dishes.

The leaves are resinous, leathery, needle-like and dark green. They dry well and retain their flavor. The mauve flowers are also edible and can be tossed into salads, or crushed and mixed with sugar and added to whipped cream to serve with fruit. Sprigs of the fresh herb can be added to lamb and pork dishes or even used as kebab skewers for grilling vegetables, meat, and fish.

You can try scattering rosemary over baked potatoes and grilled or roasted vegetables and fish, or it can be pounded and added to savory butters to serve with vegetables.

SAGE: A native of southern Europe, sage has many culinary varieties. The leaves are grayish-green in color and thick in texture with a soft downy "fur" growing over them. Some varieties are purple, others are flecked with yellow. The leaves dry well and are very aromatic and pungent. The flavor of sage is strong and can be overpowering if not used carefully—it tastes of camphor. It is traditionally mixed with onion and bread crumbs as a stuffing for poultry.

You can cook sage with fatty meats such as pork, duck, and sausage. Whole leaves can be dipped in a light batter and then deep-fried and served as a tasty garnish for roasted vegetables. Sage adds a good flavor to vinegar, and can also be made into herb butter for serving with grilled meat.

THYME: This is one of the great herbs in the European kitchen and it belongs to the same family as mints, sage, basil, and oregano. There are many varieties, but it is the Common thyme that you are most likely to see. It grows in small bush-like clumps. The stems are dry and woody, and the leaves grow in little groups and are aromatic, pointed oval and mid-green.

Thyme is one of the herbs that make up a "bouquet garni" (together with a bay leaf and parsley), and a very small amount can make all the difference to a dish. It is an excellent flavoring for casseroles and stews, and goes well with beef, lamb, pork, and chicken as well as mushrooms. The dried leaves have a very intense flavor and they should always be used sparingly.

Bay Leaves

Parsley

Flat-Leaved Parsley

Rosemary

Mace

Cloves

Nutmeg

Mixed Spice

SPICES

British cuisine has always used a wide array of spices, and although a wealth of exotic ingredients are used now, the following spices have been used in traditional dishes for many years.

CINNAMON: True cinnamon is indigenous to Sri Lanka. Like cassia it is the dried bark of a tree of the laurel family. Long pieces of cinnamon bark are formed into quills, rolled by hand every day until dry. The resulting sticks are thin and brittle. The flavor is woody, sweet, and very aromatic. Whole sticks can be used in compotes, casseroles, and in drinks such as mulled wine. Snap in half and infuse in the cooking liquid. You can use ground cinnamon in cakes and puddings.

CLOVES: Native to the spice islands of Indonesia, there are now plantations in Zanzibar, Madagascar, and the West Indies. Cloves are the unopened flower buds of a small evergreen tree which are sun dried. The flavor is strong, warming, and rich. They are used in sweet and savory dishes—chutneys, rich fruit cakes, and smoked hams. They are also available ground.

CURRY POWDER: The word "curry" comes from the Tamil work *kari*, meaning a sauce. To Europeans, it covers any hot, spicy Indian dish, but in India, there are many different regional *masalas* or blends, which are designed to flavor different foods. The most common blends of curry powder are *garam masalas*, which are usually made to order and will keep for three to four months in an airtight jar. The most commonly used spices in a basic powder are chili, turmeric, ginger, coriander, cumin, fenugreek, cinnamon, cardamom, cloves, mustard, and asafetida.

Different heat strengths are also available.

MACE: This lacy growth grows around the nutmeg seed. It is bright red when fresh but turns to an orange-yellow by the time it reaches market. The main supply comes from Indonesia and Grenada. Whole and ground mace are available. Whole mace is difficult to grind, and the ground sort is better as the flavor keeps longer than most ground spices. It tastes similarly warming and rich to nutmeg, although it is slightly bitter and more expensive. It is added to white pouring sauces, cheese soufflés, and cream cheese desserts.

MIXED SPICE: Also known as "pudding spice", this is a blend of sweet spices used in cakes, bakes and puddings. The selection of spices and their quantities can be varied according to personal taste, but it usually includes cinnamon, cloves, ginger, mace, nutmeg, coriander seeds, and allspice berries. If you grind your own mixture from whole spices, you'll get a richer, more flavorful result than from a ready prepared mix. It gives traditional Christmas food its distinctive flavors.

NUTMEG: The seed of a tree that is native to the Molucca Islands of Indonesia, it is now grown in other tropical countries. It is oval in shape with a gray-brown wrinkled exterior. The inside is lighter in color and hard. It is better whole than ground as it loses its flavor very quickly. Small graters are available for easy grinding. Nutmeg smells rich and aromatic. It is widely used in baking but also goes well with egg and cheese dishes, and with the flavor of cabbage, spinach, potato, and cauliflower.

CONDIMENTS

British food has a reputation for being a bit bland, but there are many sauces and condiments that help to liven things up and which have become main players in the Brits' daily diet.

BROWN SAUCE: Sold in bottles and available in many varieties, this is seen on the tables of most British cafés. The best known variety is HP, which stands for Houses of Parliament, in whose members' restaurant it is available. Brown sauce is a combination of spicy sweet and vinegary sour flavors, and it is good when served with a traditional English breakfast.

COLEMAN'S MUSTARD: The manufacture of mustard powder has for the last century been synonymous in Britain with the East Anglian based company Coleman's. Mustard powder is bright yellow, and it should be freshly mixed with water and used quickly in order to savor its hot and pungent taste. Packaged in a distinctive yellow rectangular tin, mustard powder enhances the flavor of a cheese dish or, when made up into a paste, goes well with ham.

HORSERADISH SAUCE: Roast beef accompanied by horseradish sauce is considered one of the nation's finest dishes, and the combination has been popular ever since the mid-eighteenth century. Cream-colored or greyish white, this hot sauce is made with finely grated horseradish root. The distinctive flavor is acid, acrid, and piquant. As well as beef, try this sauce with smoked fish, such as trout or mackerel

MUSHROOM KETCHUP: The company of Geo. Watkins claims to have been established in 1830 and is famous for this ketchup. The dark brown, thin liquid with its earthy, salty flavor is still presented in a bottle of characteristically Victorian shape. It is used to add seasoning and mild spice to stocks, soups, and gravies.

PICCALILLI: A bright yellow chunky vegetable pickle, this is flavored with turmeric, mustard seeds, spices, and vinegar. It was first known in England in the mid-eighteenth century and shows the influence of the East India trade, using imported spices and homegrown vegetables to imitate exotics. It was a good way of preserving gluts of vegetables. Now piccalilli is often served with cold meats and cheeses, and as part of the traditional Ploughman's lunch, served in pubs, along with pickled onions.

PICKLED WALNUTS: These became fashionable in the eighteenth century when they were used as garnishes or to enrich meat dishes. The nuts are preserved in brine and vinegar whilst they are still "green" (before their shell forms). The walnuts look black in the pickle and are dark grey inside. They are firm in texture, mildly sweet and spiced. They are still added to rich casseroles or served with cold meats.

WORCESTERSHIRE SAUCE: Lea and Perrins Original and Genuine Worcestershire Sauce is a trademark, and each bottle bears a characteristic orange label. This opaque, dark brown liquid has a sweet-sour, spicy aromatic taste. The exact recipe and manufacturing process are trade secrets. Worcestershire sauce livens up marinades, stocks and sauces; it is also being mixed with grated cheese for Welsh Rarebit (see page 96).

Brown Sauce

Mustard

Horseradish Sauce

Worcestershire Sauce

Part Three: The Recipes

Basic recipes for stock, gravy, sauces, vegetables, and pâté precede those for main dishes, which begin on page 42

Beef Stock

2 lb (1 kg) beef bones, fresh or from
    cooked meat
2 quarts (2 liters) cold water
2 onions, quartered
1 celery rib, trimmed and diced
2 carrots, diced
1 teaspoon salt
3 peppercorns
Few sprigs of parsley
2 dried bay leaves
Pinch of ground mace

Wash the bones, if fresh, and chop them coarsely. Place in a large, heavy-based saucepan with all the other ingredients.

Bring to a boil, and skim away the surface scum with a flat spoon. Reduce the heat to a gentle simmer, partially cover the pan, and then cook for about 4 hours. Remove from the heat and let cool.

Line a sieve or a strainer with some cheesecloth, and place over a large pitcher or bowl. Strain the stock through the cheesecloth and store, covered, in the refrigerator for up to 3 days. Skim away any surface fat before using. Alternatively, you can freeze the stock in small batches.

Makes approximately 4 cups (1 liter).

Beef Gravy

2 tablespoons all-purpose (plain) flour
Reserved beef cooking juices
2$\frac{1}{2}$ cups (600 ml) beef stock (see left)
Few drops of gravy browning (optional)

Blend the flour with the reserved cooking juices in a saucepan, and gradually stir in the beef stock. Bring to a boil, stirring, and simmer for 3 minutes until thickened. Add gravy browning, if using, and season before serving. Serves 6.

White Pouring Sauce

2 tablespoons butter
$\frac{1}{4}$ cup (25 g) all-purpose (plain) flour
2$\frac{1}{2}$ cups (600 ml) milk
Salt to taste

Melt the butter in a saucepan and stir in the flour. Cook gently for 1 minute, then remove from the heat. Gradually blend in the milk, then return to the heat.

Cook, stirring, until the sauce comes to a boil and thickens. Simmer for 1 minute, then season and serve as desired. Makes 6 servings.

Opposite:
Nothing beats a full English breakfast of bacon, sausage, black pudding, fried egg, baked beans, and fried bread.

Mint Sauce

1 bunch of fresh mint, washed
$^2/_3$ cup (150 ml) white wine vinegar
4 tablespoons sugar

Finely chop the mint and place in a small pitcher or bowl. Add the vinegar and sugar, and stir until the sugar dissolves. Set aside until you are ready to serve. Serve the mint sauce with roast lamb joints or lamb chops. Makes 6 to 8 servings.

Bread Sauce

$1^1/_4$ cups (300 ml) milk
1 small onion, peeled and studded with
    3 cloves
1 bay leaf
Pinch of ground mace
1 cup (50 g) fresh white breadcrumbs
2 tablespoons butter
Salt and freshly ground black pepper

Put the milk, clove-studded onion, bay leaf, and mace in a small saucepan. Bring to a boil, then cover the pan and simmer very gently for about 30 minutes until the milk is infused with the flavors of the onion, bay leaf, and mace. Remove from the heat and cool, then strain into a clean saucepan.

Stir in the breadcrumbs, butter, and seasoning. Cook over a very low heat for about 15 minutes, stirring occasionally, until the sauce is thick. Serve hot with either roast chicken, turkey, or pheasant. Makes 4 servings.

Roast Root Vegetables

2 lb (900 g) medium-sized floury potatoes,
    such as King Edwards, peeled and halved
3 parsnips, peeled and quartered
3 large carrots, peeled and quartered
    lengthwise
6 tablespoons vegetable oil
2 tablespoons all-purpose (plain) flour
Salt and freshly ground black pepper
2 tablespoons chopped parsley

Put the potatoes, parsnips, and carrots in a large saucepan, and cover with water. Bring to a boil and cook for 10 minutes. Drain and let stand in the strainer for 5 minutes, then return the vegetables to the saucepan.

Preheat oven to 425°F (220°C, gas 7). Place a lid over the saucepan, then shake the contents vigorously for a few seconds to loosen the texture of the vegetables—this will help to make them crisp. Carefully toss in 2 tablespoons of the oil and the flour, and season well with salt and plenty of ground black pepper.

Spoon the remaining oil into a shallow baking pan and add the vegetables, tossing them in the oil to coat them evenly.

Bake the vegetables in the preheated oven for about 20 minutes until they are golden and crisp. Drain off any oil and serve sprinkled with chopped parsley. Serves 6.

Creamed Spinach with Nutmeg

2 lb (900 g) young spinach leaves
2 tablespoons butter
3 tablespoons heavy cream
Salt and freshly ground black pepper
¹/₂ teaspoon grated nutmeg

Wash the spinach well and pack the wet leaves into a large saucepan. Cover and heat gently, stirring occasionally, until the steam rises. Raise the heat and cook for about 5 minutes until just wilted.

Drain thoroughly by pressing the leaves against the side of a colander or strainer. Coarsely chop the leaves, then return to the pan. Stir in the butter, cream, seasoning, and nutmeg. Reheat gently, stirring, for 1 minute until hot. Serve immediately. Serves 4.

Brussels Sprouts with Chestnuts

1 lb (50 g) Brussels sprouts
Salt
2 tablespoons butter
1 cup (175 g) canned chestnuts, drained
Ground nutmeg, for dusting

Trim the base of each sprout and discard the outer leaves. Cut a small cross in the base. Cook the sprouts in a pan of lightly salted boiling water for 10 to 12 minutes until just tender. Drain well and return to the pan.

Melt the butter in a skillet and gently fry the chestnuts for 5 minutes until golden. Toss with the sprouts and serve dusted with nutmeg. Serves 4.

Emile's Pâté

12 rashers rindless streaky bacon
1 tablespoon olive oil
2 shallots, finely diced
2 garlic cloves, finely minced
1 lb (500 g) minced veal
1 lb (500 g) minced pork
¹/₂ oz (15 g) pancetta, finely diced
¹/₄ cup (15 g) fresh white breadcrumbs
2 teaspoons chopped thyme
2 tablespoons chopped parsley
4 tablespoons brandy
1 egg, beaten
Salt and freshly ground black pepper

Preheat oven to 350°F (180°C, gas 4). Line a pâté pan or terrine mold with the bacon, slightly overlapping each rasher, allowing the ends to overhang the sides of the pan.

In a skillet, heat the olive oil and gently fry the shallots and garlic for 3 to 4 minutes until softened but not browned. Let cool.

Place the veal, pork, and pancetta in a large bowl and stir in the cooked shallots and garlic and the remaining ingredients. Mix well and then press into the bacon lined pan or mold, making sure it is well packed. Fold the overhanging bacon over the top and cover with foil to seal.

Place in a roasting pan and pour in sufficient boiling water to come halfway up the sides of the pâté pan. Bake in the oven for 1¹/₂ hours or until the juices run clear. Remove from the water, place some heavy weights on top of the pâté and let cool. Chill overnight in the refrigerator. Serve in slices as an appetizer or use in the filling for beef Wellington (see page 86). Serves 8.

PEARS WITH WALNUT AND STILTON DRESSING

Often served as a light pudding, pears also go well with cheese, particularly the strongly flavored English ones such as Stilton and mature farmhouse Cheddar. The pear's creamy taste and texture help to compliment the tanginess of the cheese.

4 small ripe pears, such as Conference
2 bay leaves
1¼ cups (300 ml) ruby port
3 oz (75 g) Stilton cheese without rind
4 tablespoons good-quality mayonnaise
½ cup (50 g) walnut pieces, finely diced
Salt and freshly ground black pepper
Salad leaves to serve

Peel the pears, leaving the stalks intact, and slice a piece off the bottom of each so that they can stand up straight. Place in a saucepan with the bay leaves and pour over the port. Bring to a boil, then cover and gently simmer for 10 minutes. Turn them on their side and cook for a further 10 minutes, until tender. Remove from the heat and leave to cool in the port, turning occasionally.

Drain the pears, reserving the cooking liquid, and place in a shallow dish. Cover and chill for 1 hour. Boil the cooking liquid rapidly for 6 to 7 minutes until reduced by half, and slightly syrupy. Remove the pan from the heat and let cool. Discard the bay leaves and leave the port syrup until you are ready to assemble the dish.

Meanwhile, crumble the Stilton cheese into a bowl and mix together with the mayonnaise, half of the walnuts and some seasoning. Cover and chill in the refrigerator until required.

To serve, place a pear on each serving plate and drizzle over some of the port syrup. Sprinkle with the remaining walnut pieces and serve on a bed of salad leaves with a spoonful of the Stilton and walnut mixture. Serves 4.

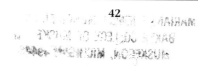

FRESH SALMON MOUSSE

The king of fishes, salmon graces the table at many dinners and parties throughout the spring and summer months. Its delicate flavor and color make it a popular addition to any menu. This light and refreshing mousse is a traditional English appetizer.

1 lb (500 g) skinless salmon fillets
1 bay leaf
1 celery rib, trimmed
²⁄₃ cup (150 ml) dry white wine
1½ teaspoons powdered gelatin
²⁄₃ cup (150 ml) heavy cream
1 tablespoon freshly chopped dill or
    1 teaspoon dried dill
3 tablespoons good-quality mayonnaise
Salt and freshly ground black pepper
8 smoked salmon slices

Garnish
Fresh dill
Lemon wedges
Quail eggs
Salmon eggs
Toast

Place the salmon fillets, bay leaf, and celery in a large skillet. Pour over the wine and cover with a lid. Bring to a boil, then reduce the heat and simmer very gently for 7 to 8 minutes until just cooked, turning the fish over halfway through the cooking time.

Remove from the heat and let cool. Drain the salmon fillets, reserving the stock, and flake the flesh. Strain the cooking stock.

Blend the salmon and stock together in a blender or food processor until smooth and transfer to a large mixing bowl. Dissolve the gelatin in 4 tablespoons of boiling water. In another bowl, lightly whip the cream until just peaking, and then fold the cream into the salmon together with the gelatin, chopped dill, mayonnaise, and seasoning, using a large metal spoon.

Pile the salmon mousse mixture into a large serving dish and then chill in the refrigerator for at least 3 hours until lightly set.

To serve, place 2 slices of smoked salmon on each serving plate and serve 2 scoops of mousse on top of each. Garnish with dill and serve with lemon wedges, freshly cooked quail's eggs, salmon eggs, and crisp toast. Serves 4.

PEA AND HAM SOUP

This delicious thick soup is often made using split green dried peas which give it a muddier color and texture. In fact, it gave its name to the great fogs or "smogs" which used to descend on London; the fogs were so dense that it was impossible to find your way about and thus became known as "pea soupers." In this recipe, the fresh green color comes from using frozen peas.

2 tablespoons butter
1 onion, diced
2$^{1}/_{2}$ cups (600 ml) vegetable stock
Pinch of ground nutmeg
4$^{1}/_{2}$ cups (675 g) frozen peas
2$^{1}/_{2}$ cups (600 ml) white pouring sauce
(see page 39)
1$^{1}/_{4}$ cups (225 g) lean smoked ham, diced
Salt and ground black pepper
Crusty bread to serve

Melt the butter in a large saucepan and gently fry the onion for 5 minutes, until just softened but not browned. Pour in the vegetable stock and add a pinch of nutmeg. Bring to a boil, then add the frozen peas. Reduce the heat and cook for 4 to 5 minutes until the peas are tender.

Drain the peas, reserving the cooking stock, and place in a blender or food processor with 4 tablespoons of the reserved stock. Blend for a few seconds until smooth. Alternatively, mash the peas and stock with a fork or potato masher.

Return the pea mixture to the saucepan and stir in the cooking stock and pouring sauce. Add the diced ham, and heat gently for 3 to 4 minutes or until the soup is piping hot. Check the seasoning, adding salt and pepper if needed, before serving with crusty bread. Serves 6.

FINNAN HADDOCK SOUP

(Snows on the Green, Shepherds Bush)

This traditional soup originated in Scotland where it was known as Cullen Skink. You can use any smoked haddock but the undyed tawny, golden Finnan haddock possesses the best flavor.

5 cups (1^1/$_4$ liters) milk
1 lb (450 g) smoked haddock
1 lb (450 g) cod fillet
^{1}/$_2$ cup (100 g) butter
2 large onions, diced
2 tablespoons all-purpose (plain) flour
1^1/$_4$ cups (300 ml) heavy cream
Freshly squeezed lemon juice to taste
Salt and freshly ground black pepper

Garnish

Carrot, cut in julienne strips
Zucchini (courgette), cut in julienne strips
Turnip, cut in julienne strips
Parsley, finely chopped

Pour the milk into a large saucepan and bring to a boil. Remove from the heat and add the haddock. Let stand for 10 minutes.

Meanwhile, cut the cod into large cubes. Melt the butter in a saucepan and gently fry the onions for 10 minutes, until soft but not browned. Stir in the flour and cook, stirring, for 5 minutes. Gradually add the haddock milk, stirring all the time until the soup is smooth and slightly thickened. Add the haddock and cod and simmer over a low heat for 10 minutes.

Transfer the soup to a food processor or blender and blend for a few seconds until smooth. Pass through a fine sieve or a strainer into a clean saucepan and stir in the cream.

Reheat to just below boiling point. Season to taste with lemon juice and salt and pepper, and then serve garnished with thin strips of carrot, zucchini, and turnip, and some chopped parsley. Serves 6.

CORONATION CHICKEN AND FRUITY RICE

This popular salad is served as part of a buffet or celebratory meal and is always well received.

2 onions, diced
1 bay leaf
2 tablespoons vegetable oil
1 teaspoon ground cumin
1 teaspoon ground coriander
1 tablespoon mild curry powder
1 tablespoon tomato paste
1 tablespoon lemon juice
$^2/_3$ cup (150 ml) vegetable stock
$^2/_3$ cup (150 ml) mayonnaise
4 tablespoons mango chutney
$^2/_3$ cup (150 ml) whipping cream
2 lb (1 kg) lean, skinless cooked chicken
Salt and freshly ground black pepper
$^1/_2$ cup (50 g) salted cashews
Fresh cilantro (coriander) leaves to garnish
Lemon wedges to garnish

Fruity rice

4 tablespoons (50 g) butter
1 onion, diced
1 teaspoon ground cinnamon
8 oz (225 g) button mushrooms, sliced
$^1/_2$ cup (75 g) no-need-to-soak dried
   apricots, finely diced
$3^1/_4$ cups (450 g) cooked Basmati rice
4 tablespoons chopped fresh cilantro
   (coriander) leaves

To make the **coronation chicken**, gently fry the onions and bay leaf in the oil together with the ground spices and curry powder for 5 minutes until just softened. Stir in the tomato paste, lemon juice, and stock. Bring to a boil and simmer for 10 minutes until tender. Press through a sieve and let cool.

Combine the mayonnaise, mango chutney, and the cooled curry purée. Whip the cream until just peaking and then fold into the curried mayonnaise.

Cut the chicken into bite-sized pieces and fold into the mayonnaise. Mix well and season to taste. Sprinkle with cashews and garnish with fresh cilantro and lemon wedges, accompanied by salad leaves and fruity rice.

To make **fruity rice**, melt the butter in a skillet and gently fry the onion, cinnamon, and mushrooms for 7 to 8 minutes until tender. Add the apricots and cook, stirring, for 1 minute. Take off the heat and let cool.

Place the cooked rice in a large bowl and stir in the cooled vegetable and apricot mixture and the chopped cilantro. Check the seasoning, then cover and chill in the refrigerator until required.

Serves 6.

KEDGEREE

This is a good example of a classic dish originating from the days of the British Empire. *Khichri* was a hot, spicy Indian dish which combined dhal (lentils) and rice with chili and other spices. By the eighteenth century, it was being served as a breakfast dish with fish replacing the dhal, and the spices were toned down to make it more attuned to the British palate. It is now a popular supper dish and is less commonly served for breakfast.

2 tablespoons butter
1 tablespoon vegetable oil
1 large onion, diced
1$^1/_3$ cups (225 g) Basmati rice, rinsed
3 cups (750 ml) water
Salt and freshly ground black pepper
Pinch of saffron
2 teaspoons mild curry powder
$^1/_4$ teaspoon cayenne pepper
1 lb (450 g) smoked haddock fillet
4 eggs
3 tablespoons chopped parsley

Melt the butter with the oil in a large saucepan and gently fry the onion for 5 minutes until softened but not browned. Add the rice and cook, stirring all the time, for 1 minute until glistening and translucent.

Pour in 3 cups (750 ml) water. Season with salt and pepper, and add the saffron, curry powder and cayenne pepper. Bring to a boil, cover and simmer gently for 12 to 15 minutes until the rice is tender and the liquid is absorbed.

Meanwhile, place the haddock in a shallow pan and pour in sufficient water to just cover it. Bring to a boil, then cover and simmer gently for 7 to 8 minutes until just cooked through. Drain and flake the haddock flesh away from the skin into bite-sized pieces. Keep warm.

Put the eggs in a small saucepan. Cover with water, bring to a boil and cook for 7 minutes. Drain and rinse the eggs thoroughly in cold running water, then peel and quarter them.

To assemble the dish, drain the rice if necessary and return to the saucepan. Gently fold in the flaked haddock, quartered boiled eggs, and parsley. Season to taste and pile on to a warmed serving platter. Serves 4.

FISH PIE WITH CREAMY POTATO TOPPING

Fish pie is one of the many familiar dishes that mix different varieties of fish and seafood. In south-west England, the pie is topped with pastry and is decorated with fish heads; it was made to celebrate the local fishing industry. This version is topped with a buttery mashed potato, a truly English staple.

2 lb (900 g) potatoes, peeled and diced
3 tablespoons milk
4 tablespoons butter
Salt and freshly ground black pepper
1 lb (450 g) cod fillet
1 lb (450 g) salmon fillet
1 bay leaf
1 lb (450 g) assorted cooked and shelled cockles, mussels and shrimp, thawed if frozen
2¹/₂ cups (600 ml) white pouring sauce (see page 39)
¹/₄ teaspoon ground nutmeg
4 tablespoons chopped parsley
1 egg, beaten

Place the potatoes in a large saucepan and cover with water. Bring to a boil and cook for 10 to 15 minutes until tender. Drain thoroughly and return to the pan. Mash the potato, using a potato masher or fork, with the milk and butter until smooth and creamy. Season to taste and set aside.

Place the cod and salmon in a large shallow pan. Pour in sufficient water to just cover them, then bring to a boil and simmer for about 10 minutes until cooked through.

Preheat oven to 400°F (200°C, gas 6).

Drain the fish, discarding the bay leaf. Remove the skin and flake into bite-sized pieces. Place in a bowl and gently mix in the cockles, mussels, shrimp (prawns), pouring sauce, nutmeg and parsley. Season with salt and pepper.

Spoon the fish mixture into an ovenproof baking dish and place on a baking sheet. Spoon over the mashed potato, making sure the fish is completely covered. Brush with beaten egg and bake in the preheated oven for 20 to 25 minutes until golden. Serve with asparagus or green vegetables. Serves 6.

POTTED SHRIMPS

(Simpson's-in-the-Strand, Strand)

Another traditional British dish, this may be served as a main course with a salad or as an appetizer. It is regarded as a delicacy, especially in north-west England. You need to use the really little shrimp for an authentic result and the best flavor. In England, these shrimp are a translucent gray color when alive but they turn brown during cooking. However, if these are not available, use regular small shrimp or even the frozen variety.

2/3 cup (150 g) unsalted butter
1 small onion, very finely diced
1 lb (500 g) peeled shrimp, thawed if frozen
Small bunch of fresh chives, finely chopped
Salt and freshly ground black pepper
Pinch of cayenne pepper
Worcestershire sauce to taste
Anchovy essence to taste
Lemon juice to taste

Garnish

Toast
Salad leaves
Lemon wedges

Melt the butter in a skillet and gently fry the onion for 3 to 4 minutes. Add the shrimp and continue to cook for 3 to 4 minutes.

Remove from the heat and stir in the chives. Season with salt and pepper, cayenne pepper, and Worcestershire sauce, anchovy essence, and lemon juice. Pile into 4 small individual ramekin dishes or molds and then chill in the refrigerator until set.

Serve the potted shrimps in the ramekins or molds, accompanied with some warm toasted bread, or, alternatively, carefully turn out of the molds and place on a serving plate on a bed of mixed salad leaves. Serve with lemon wedges and toast. Serves 8.

SCRAMBLED EGG AND SALMON ON TOAST

(The Fox and Anchor, Clerkenwell)

This dish would be served as a light lunch or for "high tea," a meal when hot light dishes are eaten instead of sandwiches and cakes. It is usually served at about 5 or 6 o'clock in the evening. However, scrambled egg flavored with salmon is also a popular breakfast dish in England and is offered in many hotels and restaurants. The flavor and texture of the finished dish depends, as with so much British food, on the quality of the ingredients used. For the best results, use organic eggs and good-quality smoked salmon, preferably wild, not farmed.

2 eggs
2 onions, diced
1 tablespoon milk
Salt and freshly ground black pepper
2 teaspoons butter
2 slices smoked salmon
2 slices wholemeal bread, toasted

In a bowl, beat the eggs with the milk and a little salt and plenty of black pepper. Melt half of the butter in a small saucepan until foaming, then reduce the heat and pour in the egg mixture.

Cook gently over a low heat for 4 to 5 minutes, stirring all the time with a wooden spoon, until the eggs scramble and the mixture is thick and creamy.

Spread the remaining butter on the toasted wholemeal bread and place on a warmed serving plate. Lay the smoked salmon on top of each slice of toast and then pile the scrambled egg on top. Serve immediately sprinkled with black pepper. Serves 1.

SALMON FISH CAKES

(Wiltons, St James's)

These delicious fish cakes combine two of the staples of English cooking—fresh fish and potatoes. Salmon is used in this recipe, but cod or smoked haddock could be substituted.

2 lb (900 g) salmon fillets
1 lb (450 g) floury potatoes, such as
　　King Edwards
Small bunch of dill, finely chopped
Pinch of cayenne pepper
1 tablespoon horseradish sauce
Salt and freshly ground black pepper
4 tablespoons all-purpose (plain) flour
2 eggs, beaten
2 cups (100 g) fresh white breadcrumbs
Sunflower oil for deep-frying
Fried parsley to garnish

Place the salmon fillets in a shallow pan and just cover with water. Bring to a boil, then cover the pan and poach gently for 8 to 10 minutes until just cooked. Drain and let cool.

Peel the potatoes and cut into large chunks. Place in a saucepan, cover with water, and cook for 10 to 15 minutes until soft. Drain thoroughly and push through a fine sieve or strainer into a large bowl.

Flake the salmon and mix into the sieved potato with the dill, cayenne, horseradish sauce, and salt and pepper. Do not over-mix; the mixture should be moist but firm. Cover and chill in the refrigerator for about 1 hour until really firm.

Divide the mixture into 12 portions and form each into a ball, using the flour to dust your hands. Flatten out into little "cakes" and dip in beaten egg, then coat in breadcrumbs.

Heat the oil for deep-frying to 400°F (200°C) and deep-fry the fish cakes, in batches, until crisp and golden, about 2 minutes. Remove with a slotted spoon and drain on kitchen paper. Serve garnished with fried parsley. Serves 6.

SMOKED HADDOCK TARTS

(Wiltons, St James's)

Wilton's Head Chef recommends that, for the best results, you use puff pastry for the tart cases as they become very light when cooked. However, the tarts can be made using regular pie crust (shortcrust pastry). You can make your own or buy the fresh or frozen variety.

6 shallots, finely chopped
3 cups (750 ml) dry white wine
3 cups (750 ml) fish stock
3 cups (750 ml) heavy cream
1 lb (600 g) smoked haddock,
   coarsely chopped
1 leek, trimmed, rinsed, and diced
1 tablespoon chopped chives
1 teaspoon wholegrain mustard
6 individual puff pastry cases, warmed
Sprigs of parsley to garnish

Place the shallots in a large saucepan and pour in the wine. Bring to a boil and cook rapidly until the liquid is reduced by two-thirds.

Add the fish stock, bring back to a boil and continue cooking until it is further reduced by two-thirds. Finally, pour in the heavy cream and boil for 5 minutes. Pass through a fine sieve or strainer into a clean saucepan.

Stir the smoked haddock, diced leek, chives, and mustard into the sauce. Bring to a boil, then reduce the heat and simmer for 5 minutes or until the fish and leek are cooked and tender.

Pile the haddock and leek mixture into the warm pastry cases and serve immediately, garnished with sprigs of parsley. Serves 6.

BAKED LEMON SOLE

(Wiltons, St James's)

Lemon sole is less expensive than Dover sole and has a distinctive, delicate flavor. If small fillets are not available, use 2 medium fillets per serving. For the decorative "clouche" of salad leaves on top of the sole, look for texture and color, such as bright green frisé, red radicchio, dark green arugula (rocket), and red and green oak lettuce.

18 small lemon sole fillets
½ cup (125 ml) olive oil
½ cup (100 g) butter
2 leeks, trimmed, rinsed, and shredded into thin strips
2 tablespoons chopped chives
Salt and freshly ground black pepper
Juice of 1 lemon
Assorted fresh baby salad leaves

Preheat oven to 425°F (220°C, gas 7).

Lay the lemon sole fillets on a baking sheet and pour over the olive oil. Bake in the preheated oven for 5 to 8 minutes until the sole is translucent and just cooked through.

Meanwhile, melt the butter in a saucepan and gently fry the leeks for 4 to 5 minutes until they are tender but retain their color.

Divide the cooked leeks between 6 warmed serving plates and then arrange 3 sole fillets on top of the leeks.

Drain the fish cooking oil and mix in the chopped chives, seasoning, and lemon juice to taste. Drizzle a little over each serving portion.

Top with a little "clouche" of a few baby salad leaves and drizzle over the remaining oil. Serve immediately while the sole fillets are still very hot. Serves 6.

SOFT ROES ON TOAST

(St. John, Clerkenwell)

Soft herring roes which are fried in butter and served on toast are perfect for eating at breakfast, a light lunch or high tea, or as a savory with a glass of port at the end of an evening meal. They are a rich buttery treat and much loved in England. If you cannot get herring roes, you could use cod roes or shad roes instead. The flavor will be similar.

Scant 1 cup (200 g) butter
1 lb (500 g) soft herring roes, still reasonably
    intact in their sacs
Sea salt and freshly ground black pepper
4 pieces freshly toasted white bread
Juice of 1 lemon
2 tablespoons chopped parsley (optional)

Melt the butter in a skillet until it is hot and bubbling but not turning brown, and then add the soft herring roes—they will curl up but don't worry. Cook for 3 to 4 minutes on each side, allowing them to brown slightly.

Remove the cooked roes from the skillet with a slotted spoon and season to taste with salt and pepper. Keep warm.

Add the lemon juice and parsley (if using) to the foaming butter in the skillet, and stir with a wooden spoon to combine with the buttery juices.

To serve, place a slice of toasted bread on each serving plate and arrange the soft roes on top. Pour over the butter and serve immediately. Serves 4.

CRAB CAKES

(The Ritz, Piccadilly)

These delicious crab cakes may be eaten as an appetizer or a main course. Fresh crab will yield the best results, but you can use frozen instead.

1½ cups (350 g) picked crab claw meat, thawed if frozen
1 teaspoon Dijon mustard
Juice of ½ lime
Dash of Worcestershire sauce
Pinch of cayenne pepper
2 bunches of scallions (spring onions), trimmed and finely diced
¾ cup (100 ml) good-quality mayonnaise
2 cups (100 g) fresh white breadcrumbs
Salt and freshly ground black pepper
4 tablespoons dry white breadcrumbs
2 tablespoons butter
2 tablespoons vegetable oil

Nantaise Sauce
1 small shallot, very finely diced
2 teaspoons white wine
2 teaspoons white wine vinegar
1 tablespoon heavy cream
4 tablespoons butter
Lemon juice to taste
Salt and freshly ground black pepper
⅛ cucumber, finely diced or scooped into balls
8 cherry tomatoes, quartered

For the **crab cakes**, mix all the ingredients together except the dry breadcrumbs, butter and oil. Divide into 4 portions and form each one into a "cake."

Place the crab cakes on a plate, then cover with plastic wrap and chill in the refrigerator for at least an hour until firm. Coat in the dry breadcrumbs and reshape if necessary.

Melt the butter with the oil in a skillet until hot. Slide in the crab cakes and cook for 4 to 5 minutes on each side until golden. Remove from the pan and drain well on kitchen paper.

While the cakes are firming, make the **nantaise sauce**. Place the shallot in a small saucepan with the wine, vinegar, and cream. Bring to a boil and keep boiling until the liquid is reduced by half. Whisk in the butter, and add lemon juice and seasoning to taste. Push through a fine sieve and mix in the cucumber and cherry tomatoes. Serve as an accompaniment to the crab cakes. Serves 4.

COD AND CHIPS

(The Seashell of Lisson Grove, Marylebone)

To many people, this is the quintessential English dish. Traditionally cooked and wrapped in paper as a takeout, cod and chips (fries) can also be plated and served sprinkled with malt vinegar or with some creamy tartare sauce.

5–6 large potatoes
Groundnut oil or vegetable oil for deep-frying
3¼ cups (350 g) all-purpose (plain) flour
2 cups (500 ml) cold water
½ teaspoon baking powder
1 teaspoon white wine vinegar
Salt and pepper
4 large skinless cod fillets (about 10 oz, or 300 g each)

Garnish
Salt
Vinegar
Lemon quarters

Peel and cut the potatoes into "chip" shapes (see the photograph opposite). Pour the oil for deep-frying into a large saucepan and heat to 180°F (350°C), or until a cube of bread browns in 30 seconds. Cook the chips for 2 to 3 minutes until almost cooked. Drain and set aside.

Sieve 2¾ cups (300 g) of the flour into a large bowl with the baking powder. Add the cold water, whisking continuously until a smooth batter is formed—it should neither be too thin nor too thick. Then beat the vinegar and seasoning into the batter. Season the remaining flour with a little salt and pepper and transfer to a plate.

Heat the oil for deep-frying to 350°F (180°C). Coat the cod fillets in the seasoned flour and then dip them into the batter. Fry in the oil until the batter is golden brown and crisp.

Remove with a slotted spoon, drain on kitchen paper, and keep warm. Fry the potato chips in the hot oil until they are lightly browned. Remove from the oil and drain well.

Serve the fish and chips, sprinkled with salt and vinegar to taste, with quartered lemons. Serves 4.

ROAST CHICKEN WITH STUFFING

This is a popular dish for Sunday lunch when many families sit down together for an enjoyable meal. Sage and onion stuffing is the traditional accompaniment and, if preferred, it can be cooled and then pushed into the neck end of the bird before roasting to add flavor to the meat.

3½ lb (1½ kg) oven-ready free-range chicken
1 small onion, halved
Small bunch of sage
3 tablespoons butter, softened
Salt and freshly ground black pepper
6 rashers of rindless streaky bacon
Fresh herbs for garnish

Sage and Onion Stuffing
1 tablespoon vegetable oil
1 large onion, finely diced
3 cups (175 g) fresh white breadcrumbs
2 tablespoons chopped sage or
   2 teaspoons dried sage
4 tablespoons butter, melted
1 egg, beaten

Preheat oven to 375°F (190°C, gas 5).

Thoroughly wash the chicken, inside and out, and pat dry with kitchen paper. Place the onion and sage inside the bird. Tuck the wings and neck flap neatly under the bird. If wished, use some string to truss the chicken and then tie it securely in place.

Place the chicken in a roasting pan, smear all over with the butter, and lay the bacon rashers across the top. Roast the chicken in the center of the oven for about 1½ to 1¾ hours, or until cooked through, basting with the cooking juices.

To test if the chicken is cooked, insert a skewer in the thickest part of the thigh. If the juices run clear, it is cooked. Drain and place on a warmed serving platter. Cover and let stand for 20 minutes.

Meanwhile, make the **stuffing**. Heat the oil in a skillet and gently fry the onion for 5 minutes until softened but not browned. Transfer to a bowl and mix in the other ingredients. Season well. Divide into 8 portions and form each into a neat ball.

About 40 minutes before the chicken is cooked, transfer 3 tablespoons of fat from the roasting pan to a smaller shallow roasting pan. Add the stuffing balls and bake in the oven, above the chicken, basting occasionally, until golden and crisp. Drain and arrange on the platter around the roast chicken.

Serve the chicken, garnished with fresh herbs, with roast potatoes, sausages, bacon rolls, gravy, and bread sauce (see page 40). Serves 4.

TURKEY AND HAM PICNIC PIE

"Raised" meat pies were developed in medieval and Elizabethan times. This delicious modern version is the perfect addition to a picnic basket.

    2 tablespoons oil
    1 large onion, finely diced
    2 lb (900 g) skinless, boneless turkey, diced
    8 oz (225 g) lean cooked gammon,
        finely diced
    Pinch of ground mace
    4 tablespoons chopped parsley
    Salt and freshly ground black pepper

Pastry
    1½ lb (675 g) strong all-purpose (plain) flour
    2 teaspoons salt
    6 tablespoons shortening, white vegetable fat,
        or lard
    6 tablespoons unsalted butter
    ¾ cup (175 ml) milk
    1¼ cups (275 ml) water
    1 egg, beaten

Heat the oil in a skillet and gently fry the onion for 5 minutes until softened but not browned. Let cool, then transfer to a large bowl and mix in the turkey, gammon, mace, parsley, and plenty of seasoning. Cover and chill until required.

Make the **pastry**. Grease a deep 8-in (20-cm) loose-bottomed round cake pan. Sift the flour and salt into a large bowl and rub in half the lard or white fat. Put the remaining fat in a saucepan with the butter, milk, and water. Heat gently until the fats have melted, then bring to a boil and beat into the flour mixture.

Turn out on to a lightly floured surface and knead until smooth. Roll out two-thirds of the pastry into a circle, ½ in (1 cm) thick. Gently ease into the prepared pan. Trim to leave a ½ in (1 cm) overhang.

Spoon in the prepared filling and pack down well. Fold the pastry rim over the filling and brush with egg. Roll out the remaining pastry to fit the top of the pie and place on top. Using your thumb and first finger, seal the edges, then make 2 holes in the top.

Preheat oven to 400°F (200°C, gas 6). Roll out any pastry trimmings to make "leaves." Brush with egg and secure the pastry "leaves" on top. Stand on a baking sheet and bake for 30 minutes. Lower the temperature to 300°F (150°C, gas 2), brush the pie with more egg, and bake for 1½ hours, covering the top with foil if it becomes too brown.

Cool for 20 minutes, then remove from the tin and place on a baking sheet. Brush the sides with more egg. Bake for 20 to 25 minutes until the pie is golden. Cool completely and then chill for at least 1 hour before serving. Serves 8.

NORFOLK PIGEON WITH FIGS AND CEPS

(The English Garden, Chelsea)

In this luxurious dish, Norfolk pigeon breasts are served in a rich Madeira sauce, topped with ceps, figs, and a slice of *foie gras*.

2 prepared pigeons, each about 10 oz (300 g)
2 teaspoons melted butter
Salt and freshly ground black pepper
8 ceps, washed and sliced
2 figs, quartered
2 slices *foie gras*, each about 1 oz (25 g)
Handful of baby red chard, washed and
   trimmed

Sauce
4 teaspoons butter
2 teaspoons olive oil
2 shallots, very finely diced
1¼ cups (300 ml) chicken stock
2 tablespoons Madeira
Sprig of fresh thyme
4 tablespoons red wine
Salt and freshly ground black pepper

Preheat oven to 475°F (240°C, gas 9). Place the pigeons, on one breast, in a roasting pan and brush with melted butter. Season well. Bake in the oven for 3 minutes. Turn over on to the other breast and return to the oven for 3 more minutes. Turn on to their backs and cook for a further 3 minutes.

Remove the pigeons from the roasting pan and let rest for 10 minutes. Discard the covering of fat and skin and remove the breasts, reserving the carcass. Cover and keep warm.

Roughly chop the carcasses and return them to the roasting pan. Replace in the oven for about 2 minutes to brown, then set aside.

Meanwhile, place the sliced ceps and quartered figs in a small ovenproof dish. Heat a frying pan-skillet until it is very hot and color the foie gras quickly on each side. Arrange on top of the ceps and figs and place in the oven for 1 to 2 minutes until the foie gras begins to melt.

For the **sauce**, melt half of the butter with the olive oil and gently fry the shallots for 5 minutes until softened but not browned. Pour in the stock and Madeira, and add the thyme and browned carcasses. Bring to a boil and cook until reduced by half. Add the red wine and plenty of seasoning, and reduce down again until thick and sauce-like. Strain and add the remaining butter.

Arrange the pigeon breasts on 2 warmed serving plates and top with the cep, fig, and *foie gras* mixture. Sprinkle the red chard on top and serve with the sauce spooned around. Serves 2.

PHEASANT AND PIG'S TROTTERS PIE

(St. John, Clerkenwell)

The filling for this delicious, rich pie is best made the day before to allow the flavors to develop.

> **3 pig's trotters**
> **Small bunch of assorted fresh herbs, such as thyme, rosemary, sage, and parsley**
> **1 whole garlic bulb**
> **2 bay leaves**
> **10 black peppercorns**
> **2 celery ribs, diced**
> **2 red onions, halved**
> **2 carrots, peeled**
> **1 bottle red wine**
> **6¼ cups (1½ liters) chicken stock**
> **2 tablespoons duck fat or butter**
> **1 lb (500 g) unsmoked streaky bacon, rind discarded, cut into chunks**
> **2 pheasants, split in half on the bone**
> **Salt and freshly ground black pepper**
> **3 onions, sliced**

Suet Pastry

> **2 cups (200 g) self-rising flour**
> **1 cup (100 g) chopped beef suet**
> **Large pinch of salt**
> **1 egg yolk, beaten**

Place the trotters in a large saucepan with the herbs, garlic, bay leaves, peppercorns, celery, red onions, and carrots. Add the wine and stock, and bring to a boil. Cover and simmer for 3 hours until the trotters are tender. Remove from the pan and pick the flesh from the bones. Strain the stock.

Preheat oven to 425°F (220°C, gas 7). Melt the duck fat or butter in a skillet and fry the bacon for 3 to 4 minutes until lightly browned. Transfer to a deep roasting pan. Add the pheasants to the skillet, season, and cook for 5 to 6 minutes until browned all over. Transfer to the roasting pan. Add the onions to the skillet and cook for 4 to 5 minutes until softened. Spoon over the pheasants with the trotter flesh and stock. Cover with foil and bake for 15 minutes. Reduce the heat to 375°F (190°C, gas 5) and cook for 30 minutes. Check the seasoning and let cool.

Remove the pheasant meat from the bones, keeping the pieces of flesh as large as possible. Add to the other ingredients, cover and chill overnight.

For the **pastry**, mix the ingredients together, except the egg yolk, and gradually add sufficient cold water to form a firm dough. Rest in the refrigerator for at least 2 hours.

Preheat the oven to 400°F (200°C, gas 6). Fill a large pie dish with the meat mixture. Roll out the pastry to fit the top and brush with egg yolk. Make a small hole in the center for steam to escape and place on a baking sheet. Bake in the oven for about 40 minutes until golden. Serves 6.

BEEF STEW AND DUMPLINGS

On a cold winter's day, nothing is more comforting than a stew. In times gone by, tougher cuts of meat were stewed for hours until tender and flavorsome.

1½ lb (675 g) lean braising steak
2 tablespoons all-purpose (plain) flour
Salt and freshly ground black pepper
1 tablespoon butter
1 tablespoon vegetable oil
8 shallots, peeled
2 celery ribs, trimmed and chopped
2 carrots, sliced
1 bay leaf
2 cups (500 ml) beef stock (see page 39)
²/₃ cup (150 ml) red wine

Dumplings

1 cup (100 g) self-rising flour
2 rashers rindless bacon, grilled and chopped
1 tablespoon chopped sage or 1 teaspoon dried
1 tablespoon chopped parsley
½ cup (50 g) beef suet
7–8 tablespoons cold water

Preheat the oven to 325°F (160°C, gas 3). Trim away any excess fat and skin from the beef, and then cut into 1-in (2½-cm) pieces. Put the all-purpose (plain) flour on a plate and season. Toss the beef in the flour until evenly coated.

Melt the butter with the oil in a large skillet and gently fry the beef with any excess flour for 5 minutes until browned all over. Drain and spoon into a casserole dish. In the same skillet, gently fry the shallots, celery, carrots, and bay leaf for 5 minutes, and then transfer to the casserole. Mix well and pour in the stock and wine. Cover and bake for 1½ hours.

To make the **dumplings**, sieve the self-rising flour into a bowl and stir in the bacon, herbs, and suet. Season well. Add 7 to 8 tablespoons of cold water and mix to form a soft dough. Lightly flour your hands and the work surface, and knead the dough gently until smooth but not dry. Divide the dough into 8 portions, and shape each into a ball.

Remove the casserole from the oven and discard the bay leaf. Arrange the dumplings around the edge of the casserole, and return the dish to the oven. Cook, uncovered, for a further 30 minutes until the dumplings are risen and firm.

ROAST BEEF AND YORKSHIRE PUDDINGS

Mrs Beeton remarked that "roast beef has long been a national dish in England," and indeed there is no finer Sunday lunch than succulent, roast beef with light, crisp Yorkshire puddings. The Victorians usually roasted their meat on the spit, but roasting at a high heat produces an equally good result. Yorkshire puddings have been eaten since medieval times. Originally, the pudding was made in a large dish and placed under the spit-roasting joint in order to catch the cooking juices.

> 4 lb (1³/₄ kg) prime joint of beef on the bone, such as ribs or sirloin, or a boned and rolled joint of ribs, sirloin, or topside
> 1 tablespoon all-purpose (plain) flour
> 2 teaspoons English mustard powder
> Salt and freshly ground black pepper
> 2 tablespoons beef dripping or white vegetable fat

Yorkshire Puddings

> 1 cup (100 g) all-purpose (plain) flour
> 1 egg, beaten
> 1¹/₄ cups (300 ml) milk

Preheat oven to 425°F (220°C, gas 7). Wipe the joint and trim if necessary. Mix the flour, mustard powder, and seasoning. Sprinkle some over the base of a roasting pan, and rub what remains into the beef fat. Leave at room temperature for 30 minutes.

Weigh the beef and calculate the cooking time: allow 15 minutes per pound (450 g) for rare beef on the bone; 20 minutes for medium; 25 to 30 minutes for well done. For a boned and rolled joint, add 5 minutes to each of the above times per pound (450 g).

Place the beef in the pan, fat side up, and dot with the dripping or fat. Bake accordingly, basting occasionally to keep it moist. Transfer to a warmed serving platter, reserving the pan juices. Cover and keep warm. Stand for 30 minutes before carving.

Meanwhile, make the **Yorkshire puddings**. Sift the flour with a pinch of salt into a bowl. Make a well in the center, add the egg, and gradually mix in the flour. Slowly pour in the milk, stirring until the mixture forms a smooth batter. Transfer to a jug and let stand for 30 minutes.

When the beef is cooked, whisk the batter, and spoon a little of the reserved beef cooking juices into a 12-cup muffin pan. Place in the oven until very hot. Quickly pour in the batter and bake for 15 to 20 minutes until well risen, crisp and golden.

Carve the beef and serve with the Yorkshire puddings accompanied with roasted root vegetables (see page 40), beef gravy (see page 39), horse-radish sauce, and English mustard. Serves 6.

STEAK AND KIDNEY PIE

(Fortnum and Mason, Piccadilly)

What could be more English than a traditional steak and kidney pie? This recipe is flavored with mushrooms and Guinness.

> 4 tablespoons sweet butter
> 2 tablespoons olive oil
> 2 lb (900 g) topside of beef, cubed
> 1 large onion, diced
> 12 oz (350 g) ox kidney, cubed
> 10 oz (300 g) flat mushrooms, peeled and cut
>   into $^3/_4$-in (2-cm) pieces
> 1 tablespoon all-purpose (plain) flour
> $^1/_2$ tablespoon tomato paste
> $^1/_2$ tablespoon oyster sauce
> $1^1/_4$ cups (300 ml) Guinness
> $1^1/_4$ cups (300 ml) beef stock
> Salt and freshly ground black pepper
> 3 bay leaves
> 1 bouquet garni of thyme, sage, and rosemary

Shortcrust Pastry

> $2^1/_4$ cups (225 g) all-purpose (plain) flour
> Pinch of salt
> $^3/_4$ cup (150 g) butter
> 2 eggs, beaten
> 5 teaspoons cold water

Melt half of the butter with 1 tablespoon of the oil, and fry the beef on all sides for 4 to 5 minutes. Add the onion and cook for 5 minutes until soft. Transfer to a large saucepan.

Melt the remaining butter and oil and gently fry the kidney for 4 to 5 minutes until browned all over. Add the mushrooms and cook for 4 to 5 minutes. Transfer to the saucepan.

Add the tomato paste and oyster sauce to the pan and stir in all the residual cooking juices. Stir in the flour and cook gently for 2 to 3 minutes. Pour in the Guinness and stock, stirring continuously until the liquid thickens slightly. Pour over the meat in the saucepan and stir thoroughly. Add plenty of seasoning, the bay leaves, and bouquet garni.

Bring to a boil, cover, and then simmer gently for $2^1/_2$ to 3 hours until the meat is tender. Let cool, and skim off any fat. Transfer to a deep pie dish.

For the **pastry**, sift the flour and salt into a bowl and rub in the butter. Add one of the eggs and about 5 teaspoons cold water to form a firm dough. Knead gently until smooth. Wrap and chill for 1 hour.

Preheat oven to 375°F (190°C, gas 5). Roll out some of the pastry and cut into thin strips. Secure on the rim of the pie dish with a little water. Roll out the remaining pastry to form a lid and stick to the pastry "collar" with the remaining egg. Crimp the pastry edges and make a small incision in the center to allow steam to escape during cooking. Brush the top of the pie with egg and bake for 20 to 25 minutes until golden brown. Serves 6.

BEEF WELLINGTON

(The Ritz, Piccadilly)

Instead of making a whole beef Wellington and serving it cut into slices, you can, if preferred, make individual ones with fillet steaks.

    3 tablespoons butter
    1 tablespoon vegetable oil
    1 lb (450 g) lean fillet of beef, trimmed
    Salt and freshly ground black pepper
    6 rashers of back bacon, rind removed
    5 oz (150 g) pâté, such as Emile's (see page 41)
    6 oz (175 g) puff pastry
    1 egg, beaten

Duxelle

    3 tablespoons butter
    1 small onion, finely diced
    2 shallots, finely diced
    Salt, black pepper and ground nutmeg to taste
    5 oz (150 g) button mushrooms, finely diced
    ½ cup (25 g) fresh white breadcrumbs
    2 tablespoons chopped parsley

Heat a large skillet for 1 minute, then add the butter and oil. When sizzling, add the beef fillet and seal quickly for a few seconds on each side. Remove from the pan, season, and let cool.

For the **duxelle**, melt the butter and gently fry the onion and shallots for 4 to 5 minutes until softened but not browned. Season and add the mushrooms. Stir over a high heat until any mois-

ture evaporates, and the mushrooms are cooked. Off the heat, stir in the breadcrumbs and parsley. Let cool.

Lay the bacon rashers, overlapping eachother, on the work surface and place some duxelle on top. Top with pâté and then arrange the beef fillet on top. Wrap the bacon rashers tightly round the fillet. Chill for 30 minutes until firm.

Preheat oven to 425°F (220°C, gas 7). Roll out the pastry into a large rectangle. Place the bacon-wrapped fillet in the center and fold the pastry over the top, sealing the long edge with beaten egg. Fold in the pastry at the sides to make a neat "parcel." Seal with more beaten egg.

Place the beef Wellington on a baking sheet and brush the pastry all over with beaten egg. If wished, decorate with pastry "leaves" or make an attractive lattice pattern in the pastry with a knife. Bake in the center of the oven for 5 minutes, then reduce the temperature to 350°F (180°C, gas 4) and cook for a further 10 to 15 minutes—this will give a medium rare beef. Cook for longer if you prefer well-done beef. Serve immediately, cut into slices. Serves 4.

ROAST CROWN OF LAMB

Roast lamb is the traditional joint served at Easter, when the new season spring lamb is at its sweetest and juiciest. To many Christians, lamb symbolizes Christ's innocence and sacrifice.

2 best ends of neck of lamb, prepared, or
  a ready-prepared unstuffed crown
2 tablespoons butter
1 tablespoon vegetable oil
1 red onion, chopped
1 tablespoon lemon juice
1 large leek, trimmed and diced
2 tablespoons chopped rosemary or
  2 teaspoons dried
1½ cups (75 g) fresh white breadcrumbs
Finely grated rind of 1 lemon
Salt and freshly ground black pepper
1 egg yolk

Garnish
Fresh rosemary
Lemon

Preheat oven to 350°F (180°C, gas 4). If you haven't got a ready-prepared crown of lamb, fold each rack into a semicircle with the bones curving outward. Press the 2 racks together and sew up each side, using a trussing needle and fine string. Stand in a shallow roasting pan and push into a round crown shape.

Melt the butter with the oil in a skillet and add the red onion and lemon juice. Fry gently for about 3 minutes and then add the leek. Continue to cook, stirring, for a further 3 minutes until the leek is softened. Place the remaining ingredients, except the garnish, in a large heatproof bowl, and stir in the leek mixture. Stir to form a firm stuffing.

Pile the stuffing into the center of the crown, packing it down well, and then cover with foil. Roast in the oven for about 1 to 1¼ hours, depending on personal taste. Remove the foil for the last 10 minutes, and baste occasionally.

Remove from the oven, drain, and place on a warmed serving platter. Cover with foil and let stand for 15 minutes before carving. Garnish with plenty of fresh rosemary and lemon, and serve with mint sauce (see page 40), roast root vegetables (see page 40), roast red onions, and creamed spinach (see page 41). Serves 6.

SHEPHERD'S PIE

Now a much loved pub meal, this potato-topped pie is one of many British recipes that were created in years gone by to celebrate local or national events. Most are potato or pastry topped and use a combination of meats and game. Another favorite is Cottage Pie which is traditionally made from cooked minced beef.

1 tablespoon vegetable oil
1 onion, finely diced
1 large carrot, finely diced
2 cups (450 g) minced lean lamb
2 tablespoons all-purpose (plain) flour
2 tablespoons chopped fresh rosemary
   or 2 teaspoons dried rosemary
1¼ cups (300 ml) vegetable stock
Salt and freshly ground black pepper
1 egg, beaten

Creamy Mashed Potato
2 lb (900 g) potatoes, peeled
3 tablespoons milk
4 tablespoons butter
Salt and freshly ground black pepper

Heat the oil in a saucepan and gently fry the onion for 5 minutes until softened but not browned. Add the carrot and minced lamb and cook, stirring, for 3 to 4 minutes until browned all over.

Stir in the flour, rosemary, stock, and seasoning. Bring to a boil, then reduce the heat and simmer for 20 minutes, stirring occasionally, until thickened. Transfer the lamb mixture to a 2½ pint (1½ liter) ovenproof dish and then set aside to cool while you prepare the potato topping.

For the **creamy mashed potato**, put the potatoes in a large saucepan and cover with water, bring to a boil and cook for 10 to 15 minutes until tender. Drain well and return the potatoes to the pan. Mash the potatoes with the milk and butter until smooth and creamy, using a potato masher or fork. Add the seasoning to taste.

Preheat the oven to 375°F (190°C, gas 5). Place the mashed potato in a decorator's (piping) bag fitted with a large star nozzle, then pipe rosettes over the lamb, making sure it is completely covered. Alternatively, spoon the mashed potato over the top. Place on a baking sheet and brush with beaten egg. Bake in the oven for 20 to 25 minutes until golden. Serves 4.

ROAST PORK WITH BAKED APPLES

Roast pork is traditionally served with stuffing and apple sauce, and this dish combines the two. The best thing about this succulent roast is the crunchy crackling. Buy the pork two days before cooking it, remove the packaging, and place on a plate. Pat dry with kitchen paper and leave uncovered in the refrigerator to dry out the skin.

> **7 lb (3–3½ kg) piece leg of pork, fillet, or knuckle end with skin**
> **1 small onion, halved**
> **1 tablespoon coarse sea salt**

> *Baked Apples*
> **8 small dessert apples, such as Cox's**
> **1 cup (225 g) sausagemeat**
> **1 small leek, trimmed and finely chopped**
> **1 tablespoon chopped sage or 1 teaspoon dried sage**
> **Salt and freshly ground black pepper**
> **2 tablespoons butter, melted**
> **Fresh sage to garnish**
> **Fresh parsley to garnish**

Preheat oven to 475°F (240°C, gas 9). Score the skin of the pork with the point of a very sharp knife, holding the skin taut and inserting the tip of the blade halfway through the fat beneath the skin. Score into thin strips. Transfer the pork joint to a roasting pan, skin-side up, and push the onion underneath the meat. Sprinkle the salt over the skin.

Bake for 25 minutes, and then lower the heat to 375°F (190°C, gas 5) and cook for a further 4 hours (35 minutes per pound/450 g) until the juices run clear. The meat will not need any basting. Drain the meat and transfer to a warmed serving platter. Cover and let stand for 30 minutes before carving. If wishes, you can make a pork gravy using the pork juices with some dry cider and vegetable stock.

Meanwhile, prepare the **apples**. Wash and core them, cutting out a little more flesh to make the central cavity slightly larger. Make a small cut round the circumference of each apple and set aside.

In a small bowl, mix together the sausagemeat, leek, sage, and seasoning. Divide into 8 portions and press into each apple. Place in a small roasting pan and brush each with melted butter. When the pork is cooked, place the apples in the oven and bake for 25 minutes until tender and golden.

To serve, remove the crackling from the pork and cut into thin strips. Carve the pork and serve each portion with a baked apple. Serve with cabbage and roast vegetables. Serves 8.

BUBBLE AND SQUEAK

Bubble and squeak is a traditional and tasty way of using up leftover vegetables. You can add any green vegetable, such as broccoli or green beans, or even cooked leeks, carrots, and parsnips to the mashed potato. It is often eaten on Mondays to cook up any vegetables remaining from the roast Sunday lunch. If you wish, you can make individual patties—just divide the prepared vegetable mixture into 8 portions and shape into little "cakes," then fry as described below.

    1 lb (500 g) leftover mashed potato
    4 oz (100 g) cooked Brussels sprouts, shredded
    4 oz (100 g) cooked shredded cabbage
    1 tablespoon vegetable oil
    1 onion, finely diced
    Salt and freshly ground black pepper
    4 tablespoons butter, lard, or white
        vegetable fat

In a large bowl, mix together the mashed potato, Brussels sprouts, and cabbage. Set aside. Heat the oil in a small skillet and gently fry the onion for about 5 minutes until softened but not browned, and stir into the potato mixture. Season with plenty of salt and pepper.

Melt the fat in a large skillet, add the vegetable mixture, smooth over the top, and flatten with a palette knife. Gently fry for 4 to 5 minutes over a low heat until the underside is golden brown.

Carefully slide the mixture on to a large plate lined with baking or waxed paper, and return to the skillet the other side up.

Cook for a further 4 to 5 minutes until it is golden brown underneath and thoroughly heated. Drain off any fat and serve immediately. Serves 4.

WELSH RAREBIT

(St John, Clerkenwell)

This traditional dish makes a splendid savory at the end of a formal evening meal. It is often washed down with a glass of port. However, it can also be eaten as a light lunch or snack, or may be served at high tea.

1 tablespoon butter
1 tablespoon all-purpose (plain) flour
1 teaspoon English mustard powder
$\frac{1}{2}$ teaspoon cayenne pepper
Scant 1 cup (200 ml) Guinness
Dash of Worcestershire sauce
1 lb (450 g) mature strong Cheddar cheese, grated
4 slices white bread

Melt the butter in a saucepan and stir in the flour with a wooden spoon. Cook for 1 minute without allowing the mixture to brown. Add the mustard powder and cayenne pepper, and then stir in the Guinness and a good dash of Worcestershire sauce. Sprinkle in the grated Cheddar cheese and stir well until it melts and blends with the other ingredients. Transfer to a shallow dish and then set aside for a few minutes to set.

Toast the bread lightly on both sides and then spread the set cheese mixture on to the toast, about $\frac{1}{2}$ in (1 cm) thick.

Place the cheese-topped toast on a grill pan under a preheated hot grill and cook for 1 to 2 minutes until the cheese topping is bubbling and golden. Serve immediately. Serves 4.

HOT CROSS BUNS

These buns are traditionally eaten for Easter breakfast or tea. Originally made from the leftover dough of the sacramental loaves, hot cross buns are always marked with a cross in honor of our Lord. These mildly spiced and lightly fruited bread buns are best served warm.

4 cups (450 g) strong white flour
$^{1}/_{2}$ teaspoon salt
1 tablespoon mixed spice
$^{1}/_{4}$ cup (50 g) sugar
2 teaspoons instant dried yeast
$^{2}/_{3}$ cup (100 g) currants
4 tablespoons unsalted butter, melted
1 egg, beaten
1 cup (225 ml) hand-hot milk

Decoration
$^{3}/_{4}$ cup (75 g) all-purpose (plain) flour
2 tablespoons vegetable oil
1 small egg, beaten
4 tablespoons milk
6 tablespoons sugar

Sift the flour, salt, mixed spice, and sugar into a bowl, and stir in the yeast and currants. Make a well in the center and add the melted butter, beaten egg, and three-quarters of the milk. Mix to form a soft dough, adding more milk if the mixture is too dry. Turn on to a lightly floured surface and knead for about 10 minutes until smooth and elastic. Place the dough in a bowl dusted with flour, cover with buttered plastic wrap, and leave in a warm place for about 1 hour until doubled in size.

Re-knead the dough for about 2 minutes and then divide into 12. Form each into a round and place apart on a large greased baking sheet. Cover loosely with buttered plastic wrap and leave in a warm place for about 40 minutes until doubled in size.

Meanwhile, prepare the **decoration**. Put the flour in a small bowl and add the oil and 4 tablespoons water to form a smooth, stiff paste. Place in a small decorator's (piping) bag and snip off the end for a hole about $^{1}/_{4}$ in (6 mm) in diameter.

Preheat oven to 425°F (220°C, gas 7). When the buns have risen, remove the plastic wrap and brush with beaten egg. Pipe a cross on top of each bun and bake in the oven for 15 to 20 minutes until risen and rich golden brown. Whilst the buns are baking, put the milk and sugar in a saucepan with 4 tablespoons water. Bring to a boil and cook for 2 minutes. As soon as the buns are cooked, brush the tops with the milk syrup and transfer to a wire rack to cool. Makes 12 hot cross buns.

VICTORIA SANDWICH CAKE

This light sponge cake is quintessential English teatime fare, and it is named after Queen Victoria. You can fill the cake with any flavor jam of your choice, omitting the cream if you prefer.

½ cup (100 g) butter, softened
½ cup (100 g) sugar
2 eggs, beaten
1 cup (100 g) self-rising flour
⅔ cup (150 ml) heavy (double) cream
4 tablespoons strawberry jam
Superfine (caster) sugar or confectioners'
(icing) sugar, to dredge

Preheat oven to 375°F (190°C, gas 5). Grease and flour two 7-in (18-cm) sandwich cake pans. Place the butter and sugar in a mixing bowl and beat together until pale and whipped in texture. Beat in the eggs, a little at a time, and then gradually sift in the flour, folding it in as quickly and lightly as possible with a metal spoon.

Divide the mixture between the 2 cake pans and lightly smooth the surface with a palette knife. Bake the cakes in the preheated oven on the same shelf for about 20 minutes until they are risen and begin to shrink away from the side of the pans. Turn out the cakes on to a wire rack to cool completely.

When ready to serve, whip the cream until it is just peaking and then spread it over one half of the cake. Spread the other half with strawberry jam and sandwich the cakes together. Dredge with sugar and place on a pretty serving plate. Serve cut into slices. Serves 6.

SWEET SCONES

These perfect teatime bakes should be well risen and have a natural "split" in the texture round the middle to enable you to twist them in half without the need of a knife.

4 cups (450 g) self-rising flour
$\frac{1}{2}$ cup (100 g) butter
$\frac{1}{2}$ cup (100 g) sugar
1 cup (250 ml) milk
1 small egg, beaten

Preheat oven to 425°F (220°C, gas 7). Sift the flour into a large bowl and rub in the butter until the mixture resembles fresh bread crumbs. Stir in the sugar and most of the milk, mixing with a palette knife to form a soft dough, and adding more of the milk if it is too dry.

Turn out the dough on to a lightly floured work surface and then knead gently to form a smooth ball, taking care not to over-work the mixture. Roll or press the dough out on a lightly floured surface to a thickness of $\frac{3}{4}$ in (2 cm).

Using a fluted $2\frac{1}{2}$-in (6-cm) round cutter, stamp out 12 rounds, gently rerolling the trimmings as and when necessary.

Transfer the scones to a lightly greased baking sheet and lightly brush the tops with some beaten egg. Bake in the preheated oven for about 12 to 15 minutes until well-risen and golden. Transfer to a wire rack to cool.

These scones are best served slightly warm with butter or thick clotted cream and some blackberry jelly or strawberry jam. Makes 12 scones.

OLD ENGLISH SHERRY TRIFLE

The Victorians called their trifle "Tipsy Cake," and it consisted of a jam sponge cake which was soaked in wine and brandy for 24 hours, and was then topped with almonds and almond-flavored custard. The version shown here has evolved over the years but still retains many of the essential elements of the original dish. For the best flavor and texture, make the egg custard yourself. However, if you are in a hurry and have no time to cook, you can use some ready-made custard. You can vary the flavor by adding a variety of seasonal fruit, such as strawberries, peaches, and apricots. A trifle is often served as a summer dessert or at Christmas.

4 trifle sponges or 8 ladies fingers
2 tablespoons raspberry jam
4 oz (100 g) cup ratafia or amaretti biscuits or
    lightly crushed almond macaroons
$^2/_3$ cup (150 ml) medium-sweet sherry
12 oz (350 g) raspberries, thawed if frozen
1 quantity custard, chilled (see page 108)
2 cups (475 ml) heavy (double) cream
Sugared almonds and raspberries to decorate

Slice the trifle sponges in half and spread each with jam. Sandwich together and place in the base of a glass trifle dish or attractive serving bowl. If using ladies fingers, spread them with jam and place in the base of the bowl.

Top with the ratafia or amaretti biscuits or macaroons, then pour over the sherry. Cover and let stand for at least 30 minutes until the sponges have soaked up all the sherry.

Spoon the raspberries over the top of the soaked sponges and then pour the custard over the top. Whip the cream until in a clean, dry bowl until it is just peaking and then spoon on top of the trifle, making sure that the custard is completely covered.

Cover the bowl with some plastic wrap or foil and then chill in the refrigerator for at least 30 minutes, or overnight, if you wish. Before serving the trifle, decorate with sugared almonds and raspberries. Serves 8.

LEMON MERINGUE PIE

This tangy lemon custard tart is a much-loved dessert and is often made with a cookie crumb base instead of a pie crust. It is best made and served on the same day as the meringue does not chill well.

Pastry

- 1$\frac{1}{3}$ cups (175 g) all-purpose (plain) flour
- $\frac{1}{3}$ cup (75 g) unsalted butter, cut into small pieces
- $\frac{1}{4}$ cup (25 g) ground almonds
- 2 tablespoons sugar
- 1 egg, separated
- 2–3 tablespoons water

Filling and Meringue

- 6 eggs
- Finely grated rind and juice of 3 small lemons
- 2$\frac{1}{2}$ cups (300 g) sugar
- 1 tablespoon cornstarch
- 4 tablespoons unsalted butter, cut into small pieces

Make the **pastry**. Sieve the flour into a bowl and rub in the butter until the mixture resembles breadcrumbs. Stir in the ground almonds and sugar, then bind with the egg yolk and water to form a firm dough. Knead gently until smooth. Roll out the pastry to fit a 9-in (23-cm) loose-bottomed flan pan. Trim the edges to neaten. Prick with a fork and chill for 30 minutes.

Preheat oven to 400°F (200°C, gas 6). Brush the pastry with egg white and bake for 20 minutes until lightly golden. Let cool in the pan.

For the **filling**, place 2 whole eggs and 4 egg yolks, reserving the whites, in a heatproof bowl over a saucepan of simmering water. Stir in the lemon rind and 1 cup (100 g) of the sugar. Make the lemon juice up to 1$\frac{1}{4}$ cups (300 ml) with water, and blend a little with the cornstarch to form a smooth paste.

Add the lemon juice and cornstarch paste to the egg mixture, and cook, stirring, until thickened and it coats the back of the spoon. Remove from the heat, stir in the butter, and pour into the pastry case. Cover the surface with a layer of buttered baking or waxed paper, and cool for 30 minutes.

Increase the oven temperature to 450°F (230°C, gas 8). Remove the pie from the pan and place on a baking sheet. In a large, clean bowl, whisk the reserved egg whites until very stiff, then whisk in half of the remaining sugar until thick and glossy. Fold in the remaining sugar and spoon the **meringue** over the filling to completely cover it. Bake for 5 minutes until golden. Serve hot or cold with pouring cream. Serves 8.

BLACKBERRY APPLE CRUMBLE WITH CUSTARD

Juicy blackberries used to grow in abundance in the hedgerows of Britain in the late summer and early autumn, and it was a popular past-time of days gone by to go blackberry picking. Due to the decline of the countryside, these fragrant berries are becoming more of a luxury.

**1 lb (450 g) green cooking apples, such as
    Bramley's
4 cups (450 g) blackberries, washed
    and patted dry
Finely grated rind and juice of 1 lemon
1 cinnamon stick, broken
$^3/_4$ cup (175 g) light brown sugar
$1^1/_2$ cups (175 g) all-purpose (plain) flour
6 tablespoons butter
2 tablespoons sugar**

Peel, core, and thickly slice the apples. Place in a large saucepan with the blackberries, lemon rind and juice, and cinnamon stick. Bring to a boil and simmer gently for 8 to 10 minutes until softened. Remove from the heat and stir in the brown sugar. Let cool, then discard the cinnamon stick.

Preheat oven to 400°F (200°C, gas 6). Sift the flour into a bowl and rub in the butter, then stir in the sugar. Transfer the stewed fruit to a $1^1/_2$-pint (900-ml) ovenproof pie dish, and spoon the crumble mixture over the fruit. Place on a baking sheet and bake for 30 to 35 minutes until golden. Serve hot with custard. Serves 6.

CUSTARD

This recipe is for a light, creamy "crème anglaise" made with eggs. A quicker version is often made with custard powder.

**7 egg yolks
6 tablespoons sugar
$2^1/_2$ cups (600 ml) milk
1 vanilla bean, split, or 1 teaspoon
    good-quality vanilla essence**

In a large bowl, whisk the egg yolks and sugar until thick and creamy. Pour the milk into a saucepan and add the vanilla bean, if using. Heat until just below boiling point, then remove from the heat and pour over the egg mixture, whisking continuously.

Return to the pan and, over a low heat, cook gently, stirring, until it thickens sufficiently to coat the back of the spoon—do not allow to boil. Remove from the heat and stir in the vanilla essence, if using.

Pass through a sieve into a warmed jug and serve. To serve cold, pour into a bowl and cover with a sheet of waxed paper to prevent a skin forming on cooling. Let cool, then chill until required. Makes about 3 cups (750 ml).

CARAMELIZED RICE PUDDING

(Snows on the Green, Shepherd's Bush)

Baked rice pudding, flavored with cinnamon or nutmeg, is a British favorite. In this version, the rice mixture is cooked in individual molds and topped with a light caramel.

1 cup (250 g) short grain (pudding) rice
1 cinnamon stick, broken
1 vanilla bean, split
Finely grated rind of 1 lemon
5 cups (1¼ liters) milk
5 egg yolks
2 tablespoons unsalted butter
½ cup (100 g) sugar plus extra to taste
2 tablespoons water
Clotted cream and cherries to serve

Preheat oven to 375°F (190°C, gas 5). Place the rice in a large saucepan with the cinnamon stick, vanilla bean, and grated lemon rind. Pour over the milk and gently bring to a boil, then reduce the heat and simmer gently until the rice is tender and cooked and the milk is absorbed. Remove from the heat and stir in the egg yolks, butter, and a little sugar to taste. Set aside.

Place the ½ cup (100 g) sugar in a small heavy-based saucepan with the water. Stir over a gentle heat until the sugar dissolves completely, then raise the heat and boil rapidly for 4 to 5 minutes until a golden caramel has formed. Pour the caramel into the bases of 8 lightly greased ramekin dishes or dariole or small pudding molds, and let stand for 5 minutes until set.

Remove the cinnamon stick and vanilla bean from the rice mixture and discard. Spoon the mixture into each mold, packing it down well. Stand the rice puddings in a roasting pan and pour in enough boiling water to come halfway up the sides of the dishes or molds. Bake in the preheated oven for 30 minutes until lightly set.

Remove the dishes or molds from the water and let stand for 10 minutes. To serve, turn out each mold on to an individual serving plate and spoon over some clotted cream. Serve with cherries. Serves 8.

DESSERTS

LEMON CURD CHEESECAKE

(The Avenue, St James's)

This is a superb cheesecake for a special occasion, made with a really sharp lemon curd, which can also be spread on scones or bread.

14 sweet oat biscuits or Graham crackers, crushed
3 tablespoons butter, melted
4 oz (100 g) puff pastry, thawed if frozen
2 tablespoons confectioners' (icing) sugar

Cheesecake Filling

3 eggs, separated
Finely grated rind of 2 lemons
5 tablespoons sugar
3 leaves of gelatin, soaked
2 cups (350 g) full-fat cream cheese
$1^1/_4$ cups (200 g) mascarpone cream cheese
1 cup (200 ml) heavy (double) cream

Lemon Curd

$1^1/_4$ cups (300 g) sugar
$^2/_3$ cup (150 ml) lemon juice
8 egg yolks
$1^1/_4$ cups (300 g) unsalted butter, diced

In a bowl, mix the crushed biscuits with the melted butter. Place eight 3-in ($7^1/_2$-cm) round molds on a board lined with waxed paper and press some of the mixture into the base of each. Chill well.

Make the **cheesecake filling**. In a bowl suspended over a saucepan of simmering water, whisk together the egg yolks, lemon rind and 3 tablespoons of the sugar until light and frothy. Remove from the heat and whisk in the gelatin.

Beat the cheeses together until soft, then mix in the whisked egg mixture. Whip the cream until it forms soft peaks. Whisk the egg whites with the remaining sugar until foamy and thick. Fold the cream and egg whites into the cheese mixture, and pour into the molds. Chill for 2 hours until firm and set.

Meanwhile, make the **lemon curd**. In a heat-proof bowl, whisk the sugar, lemon juice, and egg yolks over a pan of simmering water. Add the butter and then cook for 30 minutes, stirring occasionally, until thick. Remove from the heat and let cool.

Preheat oven to 400°F (200°C, gas 6). Roll out the pastry to form a large rectangle and cut into 24 triangles. Arrange on 2 large baking sheets and bake for 12 to 15 minutes until puffed and golden. Let cool.

Dust the triangles with confectioner's sugar and place under a preheated hot grill for a few seconds until the sugar caramelises. Let cool.

Remove each cheesecake from its mold, and spread a layer of lemon curd on top. Arrange 3 pastry triangles around each cheesecake. Serves 8.

DRINKS

TEA

There is nothing more traditional in England than a cup of tea. It is guaranteed to bring refreshment, whatever the occasion, and since Victorian times "afternoon tea," at which the drink is served with sandwiches, cakes, and scones, has become a social event either at home or work, in restaurants, cafés, and hotels.

Tea leaves of your choice, the amount depends on the size of the teapot and how strong you like your tea

Fill a kettle with cold water and place over a high heat. Bring to a rolling boil. Warm the teapot with a little boiling water for 2 to 3 minutes, and then tip the water away. Spoon in the loose leaf tea of your choice, allowing one teaspoonful per person plus an extra teaspoonful "for the pot."

Pour boiling water over the loose leaf tea in the teapot—remember that it should be freshly boiled for maximum flavor – until the teapot is about three quarters full (although this will depend on the size of the teapot and the amount of tea you are making). Leave the tea to "steep" (let stand) for 2 to 3 minutes, stirring it once to ensure that the leaves infuse properly.

Using a small tea strainer, strain the tea into some pretty porcelain tea cups and then add milk (not cream) or lemon, and sugar to taste. It is important for the best result and flavor that you always add these to the tea, not the other way round. You can add more, if needed, but you can't take it away! Serve the tea immediately, perhaps with some small cookies or biscuits, or a slice of cake.

SPICED TEA

This recipe was introduced by the "ex-pats" from India, who drank it by the gallon as a refreshing drink when the heat became excessive. You can make this without the milk if you prefer black tea.

1 small cinnamon stick, broken
8 cardamom pods, lightly crushed
6 cloves
$^3/_4$ cup (175 ml) milk
2 tablespoons loose-leaf Indian tea
White sugar to taste, if preferred

Pour $2^1/_2$ cups (600 ml) water into a saucepan and add the spices. Bring to a boil, cover the pan, and then simmer gently for 10 minutes. Add the milk and simmer for a further 2 minutes. Remove from the heat and add the loose-leaf tea. Leave to infuse for 2 minutes. Serve strained into teacups with sugar to taste, if preferred. Makes 4 servings.

OLD-FASHIONED LEMONADE

This refreshing drink is a popular thirst-quencher in hot weather and is loved by adults and children.

3 large lemons, scrubbed
5 cups (1$\frac{1}{4}$ liters) boiling water
$\frac{1}{4}$ cup (50 g) white sugar

Grate the rind from the lemons and place in a large heatproof pitcher or bowl. Cut away and discard all the white pith from the lemons, and then thinly slice the flesh. Place in the pitcher and pour over the boiling water. Add the sugar and stir until thoroughly dissolved.

Set aside until completely cold, then strain and chill until required. Store in the refrigerator for up to 2 days. Makes 5 cups (1$\frac{1}{4}$ liters).

G & TEA

This cocktail was created by Fortnum and Mason in celebration of the Chelsea Flower Show. It is very refreshing on even the hottest days and makes a perfect alternative to Pimm's.

2 heaped teaspoons Rose Pouchong tea
1$\frac{1}{4}$ cups (300 ml) still mineral water
$\frac{1}{2}$ cup (100 ml) London Dry Gin
1$\frac{3}{4}$ cups (400 ml) lemonade
Sliced apple and strawberries

Put the tea in a heatproof pitcher. Bring the mineral water to a boil and pour over the tea. Leave to infuse for about 3 minutes, then strain, cool, and chill until ice cold. To serve, mix with the gin. Fill 4 tall serving glasses with ice and pour over the tea mixture. Top up with lemonade and decorate with apple and strawberries. Serves 4.

WASSAIL CUP

At one time in England, most houses kept a wassail bowl ready throughout the Christmas festivities for unexpected guests. Carol singers carried their own cups to dip into the drink after they had sung. Drinking from the bowl was an expression of friendship, and the name comes from the Old English wes hal, which means "be thou whole."

8 small dessert apples, washed
32 cloves
6$\frac{1}{4}$ cups (1$\frac{1}{2}$ liters) brown ale
1$\frac{1}{4}$ cups (300 ml) sweet sherry
Pinch of ground cinnamon
Pinch of ground ginger
Pinch of ground nutmeg
Grated rind of 1 lemon
2 slices toasted white bread

Preheat oven to 400°F (200°C, gas 6). Core the apples and, using a sharp knife, slit the skin around the center of each apple and then stud each one with 4 cloves. Place in a baking dish and pour over $\frac{2}{3}$ cup (150 ml) brown ale. Bake for 30 minutes, basting occasionally until tender. Pour the remaining ale into a large saucepan with the sherry, spices, and lemon rind. Heat through, without boiling, until really hot.

To serve, cut the toast and apples into small pieces. Ladle the punch into punch glasses or mugs and float the pieces of toast and apple on the top. Serves 8.

PIMM'S

This amber-colored drink—with all its trimmings—is one of the most summery and pleasant English drinks. A different spirit is used in each variety of Pimm's; the classic Number 1 contains gin, whilst others contain whisky, rum, or brandy.

2 cups (475 ml) Pimm's No. 1
1$\frac{1}{4}$ cups (300 ml) chilled dry champagne
1$\frac{1}{4}$ cups (300 ml) chilled lemonade
1 small orange, thinly sliced and halved
1 small lemon, thinly sliced
Few sprigs of mint
Few thin strips of cucumber skin
Few borage flowers, if available

In a pitcher, combine the Pimm's, champagne, and lemonade. Add enough ice to chill the mixture. To serve, pour into tall, clear glasses, and garnish each with orange and lemon slices, a sprig of mint, a strip of cucumber skin and borage, if using. Serves 8.

MULLED WINE

This is traditionally served as a warming "toddy" at outdoor parties on cold winter evenings or during Christmas time.

To pack an extra punch, pour a little brandy into the base of each tumbler before ladling over the hot wine.

1/2 teaspoon ground ginger
6 cloves
1 cinnamon stick, broken
Pinch of grated nutmeg
$\frac{3}{4}$ cup (175 g) sugar

1 orange, scrubbed and sliced
1$\frac{1}{4}$ cups (300 ml) water
A bottle of red wine, such as red Bordeaux

Place all the spices in a large saucepan with the sugar, half the orange, and the water. Bring to a boil, remove from the heat, and set aside to infuse for 1 hour.

Just before serving, pour in the wine and heat gently, without boiling. Strain and serve hot, poured into heatproof punch glasses, tumblers, or mugs with the remaining orange slices to float. Serves 8.

SOURCES & RESTAURANTS

BAKER AND SPICE
46 Walton Street
London SW3
Tel: 020 7589 4734
One of the most impressive bakeries in London. Small premises, but make their own bread in brick ovens. Many varieties of bread sold as well as biscuits and salads.

BRICK LANE
Whitechapel, London E1
This is the place to try the best curries in town, or if you would like to make one for yourself—the area is brimmed full of stores that sell a wide range of Asian grocery items and fresh foods.

BRIXTON MARKET
Electric Avenue, Pope's Road, Brixton Station Road, Atlantic Road
London SW9
Offers a wide range of global cuisine especially Caribbean and African foodstuffs, fruits and vegetables. Specialist fishmongers and butchers. Daily market, except Sunday.

CHINATOWN
Central London, around Gerrard Street
London WC2
This is the main place to buy Oriental ingredients. There are many small shops, supermarkets and restaurants in the surrounding streets offering a wide range of produce.

HARRODS, FOOD HALLS
97–135 Brompton Road
London, SW1X 7L
Tel: 020 7261 0456
In the basement of the world's most famous department store can be found all manner of luxury goods and delicacies from cheeses and breads to caviar and champagne.

LEADENHALL MARKET
Whittington Avenue, off Gracechurch Street London EC3
This attractive Victorian arcade now in the shadow of the Lloyds building contains upmarket butchers, fishmongers and game suppliers. Open Monday to Friday.

PAXTON AND WHITFIELD
93 Jermyn Street
London SW1
Tel: 020 7930 0259
www.cheesemongers.co.uk
A highly regarded cheese merchants particularly well-known for its Stilton. This picturesque shop is situated amongst a select street of shops and restaurants.

PORTOBELLO MARKET
Portobello Road
London W10 and W11
Golborne Road
London W10
This is a world-famous market selling a whole range of foods as well as antiques and bric-a-brac. Organic market on Thursdays. Open daily, except Sundays.

SIMPLY SAUSAGES
Harts Corner
341 Central Markets
Farringdon Street
London EC1
Tel: 020 7329 3227

Next to Smithfield meat market, this shop sells over 40 different seasonal sausages including vegetarian and seafood varieties.

SMITHFIELD CENTRAL MARKET
Farringdon Street
London EC1
The main buying action starts here very early in the morning, but around and about the central markets there are plenty of butchers shops selling a wide range of meat and poultry and very reasonable prices.

SPITALFIELDS MARKET
Commercial Street, between Lamb Street and Brushfield Street
London E1
Occupying the old wholesale fruit and vegetable market, this market is truly up to date with a bent towards an alternative life-style. Organic market : Friday and Sunday.

THOMAS GOODE
19 South Audley Street
London W1
Tel: 020 7499 2823
www.thomasgoode.co.uk
A grand old institution selling a wide range of china, glass, silverware, cutlery and linen. Sells exclusive designs favored by royalty.

THE AVENUE
7–9 St James's Street
London, St James's, SW1A 1EE
Tel: 020 7321 2111
A stunning restaurant and bar in the
West End, serving 'progressive modern
European food.

BALLS BROTHERS
Hay's Galleria,
Tooley Street,
London Bridge, London, SE1 2HD
Tel: (0)20 7407 4301
A high-quality seafood restaurant set
in Hay's Galleria–a converted Victorian
Wharf close to London Bridge.

CAFE LAZEEZ
21 Dean Street,
Soho, London, W1V 5AH
Tel: 020 7434 9393
Anglo-Indian cuisine served in a stylish,
upmarket restaurant attached to one of
London's theatres.

THE CHURCHILL ARMS
119 Kensington Church Street
Kensington, London W8
Tel: 020 7727 4242
Superb Thai cuisine served in the comfort
of a traditional English pub.

THE ENGLISH GARDEN
10 Lincoln Street
Chelsea, London SW3 2CS
Tel: 020 7584 7272

FORTNUM & MASON
The Fountain Restaurant
181 Piccadilly, London W1A 1ER
Tel: 020 7973 4140

Modern traditional British food with
colonial influences set within London's
most famous grocery store. Murals depict-
ing the Travels of Mssrs Fortnum & Mason
adorn the walls of this stylish restaurant.

THE FOX & ANCHOR
115 Charter House Street,
Clerkenwell, London EC1M 6AA
Tel: 020 7253 5075
A traditional market pub near Smithfield
Market, is the best place to have a full
English breakfast and a pint at 7am. Also
very popular for City lunchtime diners.

THE RITZ
150 Piccadilly
Piccadilly, London W1J 9BR
Tel: 020 7493 8181
The magnificent Ritz restaurant is one
of the most beautiful dining rooms in the
world. Less formal luncheons and teas are
also available.

ST. JOHN
26 St. John's Street,
Clerkenwell, London EC1M 4AY
Superb 'Nose to tail eating' (enjoying the
innards and extremities of the beast) can
be enjoyed at this award winning bar,
bakery and restaurant.

SEASHELL OF LISSON GROVE
49–51 Lisson Grove
Marylebone, London NW1 6UH
Thought to be the best fish&chips in
London, to take away or be enjoyed in
the restaurant.

SIMPSON'S-IN-THE-STRAND
100 Strand,
Strand, London WC2R 0EW
Tel: 020 7836 9112
For over 150 years Simpson's has served
classic roasts from ornate silver-domed
trolleys—a bastion of British food.

SNOWS ON THE GREEN
166 Shepherds Bush Road,
Shepherds Bush, London W6 7PB
Tel: 020 7603 2142
The main buying action starts here very
early in the morning, but around and
about the central markets there are
plenty of butchers shops selling a wide
range of meat and poultry and very
reasonable prices.

MR WING
242–244 Old Brompton Road,
Earls Court, London SW5
Tel: 020 7373 6606
Well-known Chinese restaurant famous as
much for its funky stylish atmosphere as
well as its superb food.

WILTONS
55 Jermyn Street
St James's, London SW1Y 6LX
Tel: 020 7629 9955
Originally opened in 1742, Wiltons is the
epitome of traditional fine English dining.

INDEX